# LABAN FOR ALL

JEAN NEWLOVE was invited at the age of eighteen to dance for Rudolf Laban and as a result he asked her to train with him and become his personal assistant. In this role she worked with Laban on a variety of projects, including work in industry in World War II. She worked with Joan Littlewood for fifteen years at Theatre Workshop where the value of Laban's work was recognised. Alongside giving daily movement classes to the company, she choreographed productions and performed as a dancer and actor – her work including *The Hostage, The Quare Fellow, Fings Ain't Wot They Used T' Be, A Taste of Honey* and *Oh What a Lovely War*. She travelled widely with Theatre Workshop in Europe giving workshops in Laban's work. and received awards for her work in Poland and Russia.

She co-founded the East 15 Acting School and developed her own teaching of actors and dancers through masterclasses and summer schools. She was invited with John Dalby in 2000 to work with actors in San Francisco and the following year to Cuba, where Jean returned in 2003 to run an intensive workshop at the National Contemporary Dance School in Havana. She has subsequently been invited to work there on a regular basis. Her first book. *Laban for Actors and Dancers* was first published in 1993 by Nick Hern Books and remains in constant demand.

JOHN DALBY is a musician and an actor who started his career at the Bristol Old Vic, where he acted, composed music and painted scenery. Later, he became the first musical director of the London Academy of Music and Dramatic Art where he worked alongside the voice teacher Iris Warren. At this time he met the dancer and choreographer Geraldine Stephenson, who introduced him to Laban and with whom he ran Laban courses and performed recitals culminating in an Elizabethan masque presented to the Queen. In recent years he has collaborated with Jean Newlove on Laban courses and summer schools.

Besides teaching in many parts of the world, he has always worked as a performer, making his first appearance on television playing Gershwin's *Rhapsody in Blue*. He took over from Dudley Moore in *Beyond the Fringe* and wrote and appeared in several successful musicals and revues. His film work includes *Death on the Nile, Evil Under the Sun, The Mirror Crack'd* and *A Passage to India*. He wrote ballet music for the choreographer Sir Frederick Ashton, and for more than a decade was musical director for the legendary Evelyn Laye. In America he is celebrated for his cabaret performances, and his one-man show, *Colley Cibber - The Man Who Rewrote Shakespeare,* has been performed in many parts of the world. His book *How to Speak Well in Business* was published in America.

*Dancing with Dusters*

When Joan Littlewood asked Laban what attracted him to dance, he replied:
'I saw this man polishing a ballroom floor with two dusters tied to his feet.
"What a lovely job," I thought. "That is the way I shall go."'

# Laban for All

## JEAN NEWLOVE

### and

## JOHN DALBY

ILLUSTRATED BY JOHN DALBY

LONDON

NICK HERN BOOKS

www.nickhernbooks.co.uk

Routledge
Taylor & Francis Group
New York London

**A Nick Hern Book**

Published in Great Britain in 2004 by
Nick Hern Books Limited

Published in the United States and Canada in 2004 by
Routledge
52 Vanderbilt Avenue, New York, NY 10017

*Routledge is an imprint of the Taylor & Francis Group, an informa business*

British Library Cataloguing data for this book
is available from the British Library
ISBN 978–1–85459–725–0 (UK)

Cataloging-in-Publication Data
is available from the Library of Congress
ISBN 978–0–87830–180–1 (US)

Cover design: Ned Hoste, 2H

Typeset by Country Setting, Kingsdown, Kent CT14 8ES

ISBN 13: 978-0-87830-1805 (pbk)

Dedicated to the memory

of

Kirsty MacColl and David Dalby

# *Acknowledgements*

Our thanks to Sarah Aucott, Lindsay Royan and Jenny Frankel, who are part of the Newlove/Dalby team who generously gave freely of their time and who are exemplary in their teaching of the Scales, and who posed for some of the illustrations. We are grateful to Sally Archbutt and Viv Bridson for their encouragement and advice and to Denise Keir for her sound judgement on philosophical matters. Our special thanks to Nick Hern for his enthusiasm and confidence in this book, and to Caroline Downing for painstakingly checking our efforts and for nearly crippling herself by trying out all the exercises. Gratitude is also due to Laban's godson, Hamish MacColl, who has never ceased to be inspired by Laban's spiritual vision and who has been such a support in this venture. The authors would also like to thank each other for their forbearance of each other's quirks and foibles during the long period of gestation of this book.

# Contents

# CONTENTS

# *Foreword*

In writing this book, we have sought to make Laban and his works accessible and as comprehensible to as wide a spectrum of people as possible. For a man of his diversity and complexity, this was not an easy task but, like most men of genius, he viewed everything around him with profound interest and could reduce them to the simplest terms, while retaining a sense of wonder. To his all-embracing mind, no person, no living creature or plant, no object, no situation or activity was of too little significance to be worthy of his attention; for, to him, all were interlinked and were part of the world around us and, indeed, the universe.

It was Laban's firm belief that it is the birthright of every man to dance – not just trained dancers or folk dancers and the like, but all human beings. He felt that deep down in everyone's being there is a latent desire to just let go and dance – not the formal steps of the ballet or the ballroom – but just to dance for the sheer joy of it. But, as he realised, this desire is all too often suppressed by modern living and the inhibitions of modern attitudes. Of course, we all purport to dance at some time in our lives, even if it is only to shuffle round the floor at the company's annual ball, which is hardly an expression of joy and, to some, is sheer purgatory.

Joan Littlewood, the ground-breaking director of Theatre Workshop, was a great admirer of Laban and his ideas on dance and movement for actors. Consequently, she insisted on her actors being trained according to his precepts. This was soon remarkably evident, for wherever this famous company performed, either in Britain or throughout Europe, it was highly praised for its unique movement style. Early on, she asked him what it was that first attracted him to dancing. He said, 'I saw this man polishing a ballroom floor with two dusters tied to his feet. "What a lovely job," I thought. "That is the way I shall go." '

# *Laban*

Who was Laban? The question is often asked. Yet, mention the name Laban in any social circle apart from those directly connected with dance and you will probably be met with a blank stare. As for the theatre, it is surprising how many actors have never heard of one of the greatest theatrical innovators of our time. He has been described as a philosopher, a scientist, a mathematician and a theoretician, but these were only small facets of what he really was: an artist, an architect, a dancer and a choreographer and dance designer of colossal vision. But who was this man of immense charisma, who changed the course of dance in the twentieth century and revolutionised our attitude to human movement? What do we know of him? Where did he come from and why was he so extraordinary?

Rudolf Laban was born in 1879 in Bratislava when it was part of the Austro-Hungarian Empire. His father was a field-marshal and military governor of Bosnia and Herzegovina. As a boy, Laban travelled with his father from country to country where he was able to witness the folk dances of Yugoslavia, Turkey and Germany, and the ballroom dances of Vienna. Naturally, his father expected his son to follow him in a military career, but the young Rudolf was much more interested in dancing and art. After a brief period as a cadet, he became, much to his father's dismay, an art student where he encountered the wonders of the rules of proportion and the Golden Section which were to influence his work greatly from then on. After moving to Paris, he continued his studies, which included architecture, before opening his own studio where he shed his respectable background and prided himself on being a true Bohemian. He dressed in true Bohemian style and, being dashingly handsome, attracted many women admirers, which was to continue for nearly all his life, and to which he was rarely reluctant to reciprocate. In

Paris, he pursued his passion for the theatre, for dance and for mime. After experimenting with new dance forms and musical composition, he decided to devote his life to dance and movement.

Being a born teacher, Laban returned to Germany and opened a school, the first of many. In 1913, he opened his first summer school, with apprentice teacher assistants, in Switzerland. This embraced dance, singing, music and painting. Among the pupils was the future great solo dancer, Mary Wigman with whom he would collaborate many times. When the Great War broke out, Laban decided to remain in Switzerland with his wife and young family while his pupils returned to their respective countries. Within a year, Laban later lamented, the finest of his young dancers, French and German, were dead. As he said, 'They lived and worked together; they died killing each other.'

Returning to Germany after the war, he opened a school in Stuttgart where Kurt Jooss, later to form the Ballets Jooss, became a pupil. More schools and summer schools followed until there seemed to be a considerable network throughout Germany, all pursuing his ideals.

Like all good teachers, Laban never stopped learning; he studied and became proficient in being a dancer, a choreographer, an actor, a painter and a designer. Besides this, he was a crystallographer, a topologist, an architect, a pianist and a composer. Ever interested in the avant-garde, he had a brief flirtation with the Dadaists, while his compositions were played in concerts alongside those of Arnold Schoenberg. He also became a Freemason.

Between the two world wars, Laban's influence spread throughout Germany and beyond. For him, it was a period of tremendous activity and achievement. His energy and magnetism were boundless but he was rarely free from financial worry. Sometimes he and his family had to suffer the indignity of being turned out of their lodgings because the rent could not be paid. This was eventually too much for his wife who left him and later divorced him. All this, combined with acute bouts of depression, contributed to the bad health that was to haunt him for the rest of his life. As he said himself, 'Dance is my life,' which would suggest that he was not ideally suited to ordinary family life. His family was everybody who would listen, and he was convinced that everybody should dance. That was his passion. He delighted in working with amateurs and ordinary workers who would otherwise never think of dancing. As a result, movement choirs sprang up in many parts of Germany. Where other countries, particularly in Britain, had countless choirs of amateur singers that would perform with professional soloists, so, Laban organised choirs of amateur dancers and movers with professionals to lead them in performance. He sought ways to free dance from the restrictions of music, believing that the natural rhythms of the body were more inherent than metric rhythms. Sometimes his choirs would move to speech patterns, sometimes they would even dance in silence. He composed both short and full-length dance works of compelling originality, often dancing in them himself. While he was teaching and lecturing, he worked steadily at his great project, dance notation. Besides this, he wrote his books and published many articles. When funds were low, he would earn money from painting or drawing cartoons.

As well as the constant teaching, lecturing and performing, Laban held important posts in many major theatres and opera houses, including those of Mannheim and Bayreuth. He was a master at creating grand effects with a great number of people and one of his major achievements was a vast procession in Vienna, involving 20,000 participants. In 1930, he was appointed Director of Movement at the State Theatres in Berlin which included being ballet master at the State Opera. Following this, he was appointed by the Ministry of Propaganda, then under the directorship of Hitler's side-kick, Josef Goebbels, to be in charge of movement and dance throughout Germany. By then, the Nazis had a complete stranglehold on the arts and all cultural activities, but Laban, who had resisted joining the Nazi Party, hoped he could continue his work without compromising himself or his ideals. He had already found it necessary to adopt German nationality in order to work in Germany, a fact he was later to regret.

To celebrate the opening of the 1936 Olympic Games in Berlin, Laban was given the responsibility of preparing a major dance work involving a thousand participants. This would be a tremendous spectacle and was to take place in a magnificent new open-air theatre. Excitement reached fever pitch when Hitler and Goebbels decided to attend the dress rehearsal. It did not take Goebbels long to determine that Laban's ideology was directly opposed to that of the Nazis and it can be assumed that Hitler was not a little perturbed to witness the work of another man with undoubted charisma who could wield great numbers of people so successfully. Indeed, Goebbels is reputed to have said, 'There cannot be two masters in Germany,' and the performance was immediately cancelled. It was a terrible blow to Laban who was by then exhausted and ill. Shortly afterwards he was put under unofficial house arrest, his notation was forbidden to be used, his name was not allowed to be mentioned in schools and his books were banned.

One fateful night, he was giving a lecture in secret to a theatre full of his admirers and followers. Before long, someone passed him a note advising him to tell the audience that there would be a short interval before he would resume. At that, he was hustled out of the back of the theatre while the Gestapo were waiting to arrest him at the front. Ill and destitute, he was secreted out of the country and eventually got to Paris, whence he was brought to England by Kurt Jooss and Lisa Ullmann, one of Jooss's assistants and a former student of Laban's.

Jooss had wisely left Germany for England in 1934 and by now his Ballets Jooss was a celebrated international touring company, based at Dartington Hall in Devon, which was owned by two rich philanthropists, Leonard and Dorothy Elmhirst, and was a haven for artists of every description. At first Laban, who was very weak, was a guest of Jooss in his house that the Elmhirsts had built for him but, before long, the Elmhirsts took Laban under their wing. They gave him his own quarters where they encouraged him to continue working on his theories and to write his masterly book, *Choreutics*. Even if he had been well enough, Laban, being an alien, was not allowed to work in England and, when war broke out, being from Germany, he and Lisa Ullmann had to move inland, away from the possibility of giving signals to the enemy. Having neither money nor the possibility of earning any, where could they go? The Elmhirsts came to the rescue and lent them their flat in Mayfair and made sure they were financially secure. No praise can be too high for these two truly good people, but it was Lisa Ullmann who would prove to be Laban's salvation. She had already risked her life, smuggling some of Laban's papers out of Germany; the train she was on was being searched by the Gestapo who were on her trail but she managed to escape detection by clinging to the outside of the carriage. Laban always called her 'a brave girl'.

With the coming of the Blitz, many people left London and a place was found for Laban and Lisa Ullmann by the Elmhirsts in Wales. Here, they had to account for their every move to the police, but through the Elmhirst's influence, they were at last given work permits. Lisa Ullmann was able to teach in local schools which were bursting with evacuees while Laban continued with his writing. Eventually, they were able to give classes together, their presence soon attracting the attention of physical educationalists and dance teachers.

Before long, courses were arranged and lectures given. Laban, at first through ill health, could do little more than lend his presence while Lisa Ullmann often taught for six hours a day. She became Laban's mouthpiece, lecturing on his behalf, demonstrating the effectiveness of his dance notation and, eventually, translating all his books for him. So it was in the field of education that Laban's work was beginning to be accepted; the theatre, already greatly diminished by the war, was not in a fit state to receive new ideas. However, Frederick Lawrence, a management consultant who was one of the trustees of Dartington Hall, was convinced that Laban's views on movement analysis, and the fact that he could notate any movement of the human body, would be invaluable to improving efficiency and, indeed, harmony, in the industrial workforce. Collaborating with Lawrence, Laban was employed as an adviser to the firm Paton Lawrence and Company. This meant moving to Manchester where he was at last able to earn his own living. Through his knowledge of movement and effort, he was able to solve many problems including those incurred by women who were having to do the heavy work of men. Through his observations he could detect when a worker's personal movement characteristics were unsuited to the work they were doing; with a little reorganising and judiciously suiting the task to the individual, the output of workers was dramatically increased.

Thus, Laban made an immense contribution to the war effort. His collaboration with Lawrence resulted in the booklet, *Laban/Lawrence Industrial Rhythm* which was to revolutionise future work in industry and agriculture. Meanwhile, the physical educationalists and dance teachers were eager to incorporate Laban's work into their schedules. Though the war was at its most grim stage, he and Lisa Ullmann were invited to teach and give lectures at Modern Dance courses. From this, Modern Educational Dance became established in Britain.

In Manchester, Laban and Lisa Ullmann now occupied part of a large house where they started giving informal classes in the basement. At first, there were only four students, but as numbers increased, so the Art of Movement Studio came into being. At the same time, Laban-based amateur dance groups were being formed in many parts of the country. When his health permitted, Laban taught on various dance and drama courses within easy reach of Manchester as well as continuing his industrial work and his writing. Soon the Art of Movement Studio outgrew the house in Manchester, so it moved to delightful rural premises at Addlestone in Surrey, which were donated by the Elmhirsts' son, William, who was a student there. By this time, the Studio had a formidable faculty of assistants who, led by Lisa Ullmann, were instrumental in establishing Laban's work in Britain. It was in this pleasant atmosphere that Laban spent his final years and, when he died in 1958, he could rest assured that his work would be carried on and would flourish.

Laban's philosophy was based on the belief that the human body and mind are one and inseparably fused. We cannnot escape the fact that mankind is part of the natural world and, ideally, conforms to the laws of nature, recalling the great days of Ancient Greece, when all education was divided into the categories of 'Music' and 'Gymnastic', stressing the importance of the link between the culture of the mind and that of the body. This relatedness seems self-evident and makes the Art of Movement a coherent and logical study.

The legacy Laban left us is immeasurable and far reaching: in dance, in the theatre, in physical education, in industry, in agriculture and in therapy. Many people are influenced by his work without even realising the fact. Perhaps his greatest achievement was to prove, beyond any doubt, that we can all find pleasure, even ecstasy, in our ability to move.

# Some Useful Terms and Expressions

For those who are new to Laban, there are certain terms and expressions which he used and which should be explained to help in the understanding of his work.

**Stance.** For the purposes of this book, this simply means standing in a state of preparedness before embarking on an exercise or movement sequence. The feet should be slightly apart, positioned approximately below the shoulders, with the weight equally distributed and the arms hanging loosely at the sides.

**Kinesphere** is the personal space surrounding each one of us and extends as far as we can reach in any direction. Outside our kinesphere is general space; whenever we move, we take our kinesphere with us and displace the general space. If we turn round, our kinesphere turns with us while the general space remains the same. Sometimes, another person's kinesphere gets too close for comfort!

**The Dimensional Cross** is the basis of Laban's theory of movement because, as he observed, we move in a three-dimensional way; we can reach high and low, from side to side and forwards and backwards.

**Pathways and Trace Forms.** A pathway is the route of a single movement traced by the body or part of it (such as an arm or leg) from one point to another. A trace form is the *shape* a movement makes in the air. For instance, if you draw a circle in the air, that is a continuous trace form; if you draw a square, that is a trace form consisting of four pathways.

**Monolinear and Polylinear Movements.** A monolinear movement is the flow through successive joints in a continuous sequence i.e. Shoulder, elbow, wrist and hand. A polylinear movement is where all the joints move at once.

**Levels** and **Zones.** It is generally accepted that in movement there are three levels: high, medium and deep. The high level is where the arms reach above the head; the medium level is the area surrounding the waist; the deep level is towards the floor. There are five main zones. When the body is held in an upright or vertical position, these zones can be clearly identified. There is the zone of the head, the two zones of the arms and the two zones of the legs. The arms can each circle in expansive, sweeping movements in a variety of directions, such as, forward, backward, sideways and diagonally at high and medium level. The legs can also circle, but their zonal areas, whilst following similar directions, travel in the deep to medium levels. These are the natural areas for the limbs. However, those who are double-jointed or particularly supple can lift their feet into the high zone with ease!

**Continuum**. This is used in the dimensional context to mean an imaginary line travelling from one extreme to another.

**Stable** and **Labile.** Stable implies stability and balance, whereas labile implies a lack of equilibrium or being off balance.

**Counter-tension** means one tension in opposition to another. For example, if your right leg were fully extended behind you and your left arm were fully extended in front of you, there should be an equal counter-tension between them.

**Gesture.** This is a term usually reserved for movements of the arms but can equally refer to the movements of a leg, provided it doesn't take any weight on it, such as a kick. Gestures can also be made with the head and also the shoulders.

**Demi-pointe**. This term is used when the heel of the supporting foot is raised off the floor and the weight is taken on the ball of the foot.

# *Steps*

Laban was so much a pioneer of freedom of movement in body and mind that it is sometimes assumed that he set no value on steps at all and that any old foot would do. This is because, for him, the step was part of a whole movement and not a separate entity. He certainly did not think of dance in terms of steps and counts. When he directed movement or dance he didn't emphasise steps but somehow the steps emerged, and they were right. This was because everyone knew where to put their weight. Steps are all to do with changing the weight from one foot to another. But what is a step? And for that matter, what is a half-step? So many would-be good dancers are held back by an inability to pick up steps, and those who get left behind in a class by the quick ones soon get discouraged. Laban's clear explanation of steps and half-steps should solve the problem and will be just as useful to those who pick up steps easily when they have to teach those who can't.

### *The half-step*

● Take up stance with your feet slightly apart and your weight equally distributed. This is called a **closed position**. Step forward with your right foot, changing your weight from both feet to your right foot only. To make quite sure your weight is only on your right foot, lift your left foot very slightly off the floor. This is called a **half-step**. Now bring your left foot forward to join your right foot in stance and take your weight equally on both feet. This is another **half-step**. The routine is always the same: a **half-step** moves from a **closed position** to an **open position** or from an **open position** to a **closed position**. Try this again, quite slowly, concentrating more on your weight transference than on your feet so that your whole body is involved. When you feel quite sure of it, perform the exercise with your left foot stepping forward, lifting your right foot slightly off the floor to check that your weight is only on your left foot – a **half-step**. Now bring your right foot to join the left in stance and your weight equally on both feet – another **half-step**. Practise these movements several times until you can speed them up a little, then you can step from one closed position to another in other various directions, such as backwards, sideways and diagonally.

### The whole-step

● From stance, take a **half-step** forward onto the left foot and make sure your weight is on your left foot only. This is called an **open position** *from which your* **whole-step** *will start*. Now bring your right foot forward to pass your left foot and, stepping ahead of it, transfer your weight onto it. This is another **open position**. Moving from one **open position** to another **open position** is a whole-step. Repeat these **open positions** (as in normal walking), and be very conscious of the complete transference of your weight from one foot to the other. Finish your walking with a **half-step** returning you to stance. Remember that if the foot or leg is moved without taking weight, it is known as a **gesture**.

Try these time-honoured step sequences but don't just do them with your feet. Let the movement flow through your whole body.

### 1. Sideways half-step

● This involves a sideways **half-step** and a **gesture**. From stance, take a **half-step** to the right with your right foot and take your weight on it. Bring your left foot over to join it in a brief **gesture**, without taking any weight on it. Return your left foot to its former position and take your weight on it and bring your right foot over to join it in a brief **gesture**. Do this in a continuous easy oom-pah rhythm and you have the simple movement of countless final chorus line-ups.

### 2. Half-step chain

● From stance, take a **half-step** to the right with your right foot and take your weight on it. Bring your left foot over to join it and transfer your weight onto it, making another **half-step**. Continue the process so that you move sideways across the floor in **half-steps**. Finish in stance and return, reversing the process.

### 3. Step-and-point and step-and-kick

● From stance, take a **half-step** to the right with your right foot and take your weight on it. Bring your left foot to cross in front of the right, and tap the floor in a **gesture** before returning it to its original position. Take your weight on your left foot and bring your right foot to cross in front of it, and tap the floor in a **gesture**. Do a continuous step-tap sequence of this, which also goes well with an easy oom-pah rhythm. Having mastered this, instead of tapping the crossed-over foot, make it into a kick, getting ever higher and higher and accenting the second beat (the kick) into oom-PAH, oom-PAH.

### 4. Double sideways half-step

● This involves travelling sideways in three **half-step**s and a **gesture**. From stance, take a **half-step** to the right with your right foot and take your weight on it. Bring your left foot over to join it and transfer your weight onto it. Take another **half-step** to the right with your right foot and take your weight on it. Bring your left foot over to join it in a brief **gesture**, without taking weight on it. Return your left foot to its last position and take weight on it. Bring your right foot over to join it and transfer your weight onto it. Take another **half-step** to the left with your left foot and bring your right foot over to join it in a brief **gesture**. In this way you have moved your body twice to the right and twice to the left, in an even rhythm. Repeat this for as long as you like and then add some variations, like kicks.

### 5. In Front, Behind

● From stance, take a **whole-step** to the left with your right foot crossing in front of your left and take your weight on it. Then take a **whole-step** to the left with your left foot and take your weight on it. Now take another **whole-step** to the left with your right foot crossing behind the left foot and take your weight on it. Then again, take a **whole-step** to the left with your left foot and take your weight on it. Continue this movement in an even rhythm across the room in a slight zig-zag pattern, letting your body swivel with the steps. In effect, when moving to the left it is the right foot (and leg) that steps in front and behind the left. Make the return journey to the right, starting with your left foot crossing in front of the right.

### 6. Step-ball-change

● This a real old chestnut. From stance, take a **half-step** to the right with your right foot and take your weight on it. Quickly bring your left foot over to join it, briefly taking your weight on the ball of that foot before your right foot takes another **half-step** to the right and taking weight again. This creates a dotted rhythm:

Reverse the procedure, starting with your left foot.

From these examples, you can attempt all kinds of interesting floor patterns. For instance, try taking a **half-step** backwards with your right foot, followed by two **whole-steps** backwards (left then right) and close on a **half-step,** as you turn to the right. Repeat this procedure three times and you will find yourself back facing the front having turned in a square. Repeat the procedure, starting with a **half-step** backwards with your left foot.

● Imagine you are standing in the middle of a six foot square, marked on the floor. Using the corners as a guide, from stance, take a **half-step** towards the right front corner with your right foot and take your weight on it, immediately followed by a **whole-step** towards the left front corner with your left foot, then bring your right foot close to your left in stance. Now take your left foot back in a **half-step** towards the left back corner of the square, taking your weight on it, the right foot immediately following with a **whole-step** towards the right back corner before your left foot joins it once again in stance. Using your whole body, and with a certain lilt to it, you will have done the basic steps of the waltz!

# Why Plato?

Whether we like it or not, it is geometry that gives us a tangible image of space, be it a straight line, a square, a rectangle or any other shape that many of us learnt to hate at school. The rooms we live in are geometrical shapes, and we live our lives in them according to the position of the doors and windows. Without geometry of some sort, space is just an immeasurable void and, when we consider the mysteries of outer space, it is beyond the comprehension of most of us.

Today, with our increasing knowledge of the boundless universe, it is daunting to contemplate man (ourselves) in relation to the cosmos, but that was one of the driving forces behind Laban's quest to discover the basic laws of human bodily movement. This quest led him on a long course of study and research in the arts and sciences which eventually brought him to the Dialogues of Plato, in particular the 'Timaeus'. But before we discuss Plato, let us briefly consider his predecessor (that unloved figure from our schoolrooms) Pythagoras. Pythagoras was a remarkable Greek philosopher who lived in the 6th century B.C. Apart from being a mathematician, he was an accomplished musician and played the seven stringed harp with great skill. He became fascinated by the mathematical correspondence between the different lengths and tensions of the strings and the musical intervals they produced. These harmonies, he was convinced, corresponded to nature and contained a formula of universal application. What is more, he could see a parallel in this harmony and the movements of the planets. It is rather pleasant to picture him sitting under a clear night sky, plucking the seven strings and comparing their ratios with the movement of the seven planets that were then known. From this was born the idea of the music of the spheres, but Plato, a follower of Pythagoras, was not content with aural harmony but sought to make harmony visible in three dimensions in the form of the five perfect geometrical solids. Influenced by Pythagoras in reducing everything to first principles, Plato took the four elements of which all matter was thought to be composed – earth, air, fire and water – and reduced them to triangles. From these fundamental triangles could be made four, perfect geometrical solids, perfect, because each one consisted of planes or facets that were identical. These were, and still are: the tetrahedron, the hexahedron or cube, the octahedron and the icosahedron, and were what Plato considered the 'best' figures for the purpose of explaining how the universe was put together. The fifth geometrical solid, the dodecahedron, which emerged later and most nearly resembled a sphere, Plato regarded as representing the cosmos.

Taken in the order of the number of facets they possess, the five solids are:

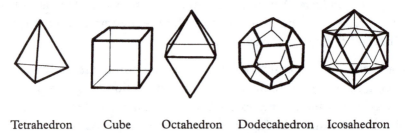

Tetrahedron    Cube    Octahedron    Dodecahedron    Icosahedron

Figure 1: The five Plato solids or crystals

Of the five perfect solids (or crystals, as Laban preferred to call them), the tetrahedron has the least number of sides or facets, consisting of four equilateral triangles, making four points (or vertices). Plato identified the tetrahedron with the element of fire. The hexahedron, or cube, has six equal sides with eight vertices. We see examples of cubes around us every day from boxes to sugar lumps, and, if we throw dice, we certainly know the feel of a cube in our hands. The cube is the 'stable' solid that Plato identified with earth. You may wonder why the pyramid is not a perfect solid – its sides may be equilateral triangles but its base is square. However, clap two pyramids together at the base and you have the perfect octahedron with eight equal facets and six vertices. Plato identified the octahedron with the element of air. The fourth solid is the dodecahedron with twelve, identical pentagonal facets and twenty vertices. This very nearly resembles a sphere and so Plato assigned no elemental quality but identified it with the cosmos as a whole. The fifth solid is the icosahedron, a beautiful shape with twenty identical facets and twelve vertices. This, Plato identified with water. Sceptical as we might be of all this, it is significant that modern scientific research into the structure of the atom and the crystal, reveals that Plato's teaching, arrived at by deduction and intuition (he had no scientific instruments to help him), contained an astonishing degree of accuracy.

Science has shown that the fundamental shape which occurs in every form of inorganic life is the triangle. Since the beginning of civilisation, the triangle has dominated every concept of the subject of proportion. Leonardo da Vinci was fascinated by Plato's theory that in three-dimensional space there were only five regular and perfect solids. Solids that intersected and interacted in such a way as to produce all the various discords and harmonic resolutions which are found in space within the universe. And Laban, like Plato before him, relying on his intuition and supreme vision, rather than scientific proof, devised a series of connections between the mathematical crystal shape and the human body on which he based a solid foundation for the practice of movement and dance.

Some of us may wonder what seemingly inanimate crystals have got to do with our own personal movement and may consider all this reference to our being part of the cosmos as so much wishful-thinking tosh, but crystals are composed of molecules and so are we. Science has proved that all matter is made of molecules and that they are in a continual state of rapid and random motion. The molecules are held in relatively fixed positions in a regular array in what is called the crystalline structure of the solid. We also know that a crystal is a form in which molecules regularly cluster together according to their affinity: it has a definite internal structure with the external form enclosed by a number of symmetrically-arranged plane faces. And, if we ourselves are made of atoms and molecules, it is thrilling to learn with the authentication of science that there are carbon atoms in every cell of our bodies and that these atoms originated in space, pumped out by dying stars, a long, long time ago, before being re-processed in the biosphere, and eventually becoming part of the structure of all life on earth. Science has at last become poetical when it informs us that we are all made of stardust.

And what of carbon itself? For a long time, diamond and graphite have been accepted as the only earthly forms of pure carbon. However, late in the 20th century, the discovery of a third form of pure carbon was a sensational event. For years, rival chemists in their laboratories had vied with each other to analyse the composition of the carbon molecule and their various machines would constantly come up with the mysterious number of 60. Why 60? And 60 what? It was Sir Harry Kroto who won the Nobel Prize for Chemistry in 1996 for discovering what is now known as the carbon 60 molecule – a perfect sphere, a billionth of a metre wide, its surface consisting of 20 hexagons, 12 pentagons and – wait for it – 60 vertices! To bring us down to earth, this shape is identical to the shape and construction of the modern football.

Nature loves the perfect symmetry of the sphere; it is seen in viruses and all sorts of microscopic sea creatures. To Plato, the sphere symbolised the whole cosmos in that it separated order from chaos, the five perfect solids representing universal order. The sun, the moon and the planets were all spheres (and even then it was suspected that the earth itself may be a sphere) all revolving in concentric circles, the circle being the perfect pathway. Of course, it must be remembered that Plato would never have seen a molecule and if his pronouncements on the proportional inter-relations between all forms of life in his *Timaeus* have long been super-seded by over 2000 years of scientific discovery and research, the fact is that the five perfect solids remain as perfect today as they were then and, what is more, they work for *us*, now. This is what so inspired Laban and, remembering that he studied crystallography, we can understand him perfectly when he said, 'In the growth of crystals (and what is not a crystal?); in the life of plants and in the weave of boundless existence which we call the cosmos, no other driving power can be recognised but the one that also creates the dance.'

# I

# *Using the Five Crystals*

Laban much preferred the word 'crystals' to 'solids', not only because it sounded more poetic but because the image of a transparent crystal lends itself more readily to the idea of stepping inside it and moving around in its space. Ideally, each crystal should be the right size in the imagination for the person moving inside it, who should be able to reach all its extremities.

Needless to say, human movement long preceded any notions of linking it with geometrical shapes but Laban looked upon these five multi-faceted crystals as a basic imaginative scaffolding upon which movements could be made with some precision. The personal space surrounding our bodies' reach, Laban called the kinesphere; when we are given specific movements to do within it, or wish to do them of our own accord, be it for dancing, acting, gymnastics, sport or any other physical activity, without a map, it can prove unnecessarily difficult and the result often lacking in precision. However, if we follow Laban's use of the five poly-hedral crystals as maps, placed firmly in the mind, we are able to traverse the centre as well as to explore all the corners and sides of these perfect shapes and arrive at movements that are precise and expressive in space rather than aimlessly wallowing about.

Before we explore the five crystals in movement, the following exercise should prove useful:

## *Increasing the mobility of your spine*

1  Preparation: Hold the back of a chair with both hands; stand fairly near to it with your feet slightly apart and slightly turned out. Prepare by bending your knees and make sure they remain directly in line with your feet (see Figure 2 below). 1. Tilt your pelvis forwards as far as it will go. 2. Let the movement follow through,

bringing your chest high above your hips. This movement can be equated with standing facing a wall and pressing your hips to the wall, followed by pressing your stomach and then your chest to the wall with your head inclining backwards. Lift onto demi-point as your body takes an upright position. 3. Curl your spine forwards, bringing with it your head and shoulders into a rounded position, taking care your pelvis is still tucked underneath. 4. Lower your heels and let your knees bend again and your pelvis resume its normal position. Your spine should have followed a circle – going upwards at the front and downwards at the back. With this rotary movement in mind, repeat as smoothly as possible to a count of four.

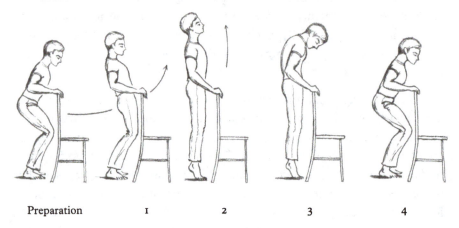

| Preparation | I | 2 | 3 | 4 |

Figure 2: Mobilising the Spine

## THE CUBE

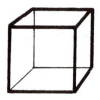

Of the five crystals, as we have observed, the tetrahedron is the first because it has the least amount of facets and vertices. It is a sharp crystal and is therefore difficult in its shape and the demands it makes. Suppose we start with the second of these structures, the cube, which Plato equated with Earth because it is the most immovable of the crystals and has a stable base (you can't knock a cube over very easily and, if you did, it would look just the same). The cube is perhaps the easiest to envisage (a box of six equal sides) and is quite straight-forward to use as a map. First of all, find a space in your room and check that you can move your arms freely in any direction without hazard (mind that Ming vase and the chandelier).

If nothing gets in your way, you can begin.

### *Imagining yourself in the Cube*

● Imagine you are standing in a large, transparent box, having sides of equal length. Take a little time to visualise quite clearly the shape of the cube around you. Feel that you can touch all four walls, the floor and the ceiling. Enjoy this feeling.

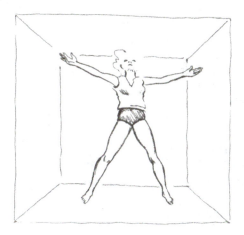

Figure 3: Standing in the cube

Standing in the centre of your imaginary cube, your head should be directly below the middle of the 'ceiling'. Reach out your arms into a wide position, right and left, and feel as though you can reach the centre of the side walls. After this, reach forward and backward, and feel as though you can touch the centres of the front and back walls. Then feel the floor of the cube with your feet and, without raising your shoulders, feel the ceiling by stretching your arms up as far as they will go. Now bring your arms down to your sides into the stance position, facing front.

Figure 4: Stance position

### Exploring the Right Side of the Cube with your Right Arm

● From stance, lift your right hand in the direction of the right, high, forward corner of the cube. You may wish to put a little more weight on your right foot and incline your body forward as you stretch for all you're worth towards this high corner. (You may wish to go on your toes but don't lift your shoulders.)

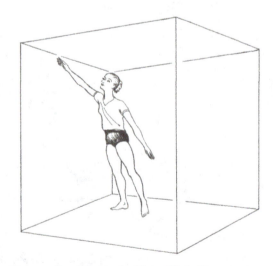

Figure 5: Reaching to the Right, High, Front corner

30

Your hand can be raised in a variety of ways. For instance, you can lift it with the palm facing downwards, like a blessing, or you can lift it with the palm facing upwards. This involves a degree of rotation of the arm. Try both ways. Now travel along the high, right edge of the cube to the high, right, backward corner. This provides something of a challenge because you must keep your body facing the front. Picture the back corner being directly behind the front corner of the cube.

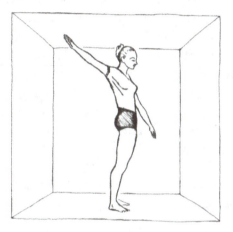

Figure 6: Reaching to the Right, High, Back corner

Continue the movement downward along the edge to to the deep, right, back corner. Reaching the back corners of the cube can only be an approximation but the points aimed for must be clearly in the mind. Let your knees bend as far as possible without losing your balance, at the same time tilt your pelvis as far forward as it will go and lift your chest before arching your back. Stretch as far as possible into the corner.

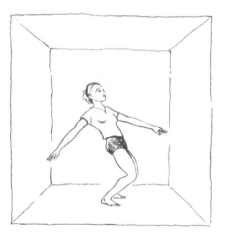

Figure 7: Reaching to the Right, Deep, Back corner

Continue to move along the deep, right edge, to the deep, right, forward corner. You will find this is slightly easier on your shoulder. Your body will now be leaning forward and slightly over to the right as it stretches into this corner. To complete the square, rise up to standing position, leaning forward with your hand and arm as it moves up this edge, into the high, right, forward corner once again.

The square you have just described in movement stretches your body on the right side as far as it is possible to go, without moving your feet. Your feet should remain flat on the floor throughout the exercise. Try exploring every part of the surface of this right-hand wall that you can reach, without turning your body or your feet, and keeping your hand flat. Your weight may have to move over to the right foot and your explorations should travel upward, downward and forward and backward and in a variety of directions as in straight lines, circles, curves and angles returning to your starting position.

### Exploring the Left Side of the Cube with the Left Arm using a different pathway

● From stance, lift your left hand in the direction of the left, high, forward, corner of the cube. As with the right side, you may wish to put a little more weight on your left foot and incline your body forwards as you stretch for all you're worth to this high corner. Continue the movement downwards, this time, until reaching the left, deep, forward, corner. Let your knees bend and your body naturally incline forwards to help your balance.

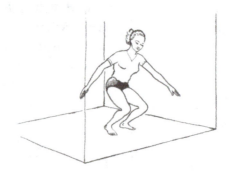

Figure 8: Reaching to the Left, Deep, Front corner

32

Continue the movement along the sideways edge to the left, deep, back corner of the cube. You will find that your hand has a natural tendency to turn outwards as it stretches to the left, deep, backward corner. From curling forward, your body will be arching slightly over backwards. Once again, it is necessary to remind yourself that you must try and remain facing the front. In other words, your shoulders should be parallel to the front wall of the cube.

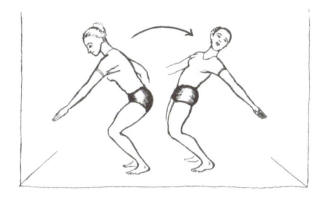

Figure 9: Moving from the Left, Deep Front corner to the Left, Deep Back

Rising from this deep position, trace the rising edge with your hand until arriving at the left, high, back corner. Do your best to make this difficult movement-change a smooth transition, with the high corner immediately over the deep one. For those of you who like a challenge, you could practise a falling and rising motion several times, making quite sure your corners are accurately placed. Continue the movement along the top sideways edge with your hand until you arrive back at your starting point. Your body will have moved from a slight arch to upright (half-way along the high sideways edge) to incline forward as you stretch upward to the left, high, forward corner. Your left side has been stretched as far as possible without moving your feet. Now try exploring as much of the left wall as you can reach, feeling it with your hand and keeping it as flat as possible. Touch every part of the wall, using a variety of shapes once again. Be inventive!

### *Exploring the Left Side and Pathway (as before) leading with the Right Arm*

● Don't say this is impossible, but it is difficult. From stance, take your right arm across your body and reach for the left, high forward corner.

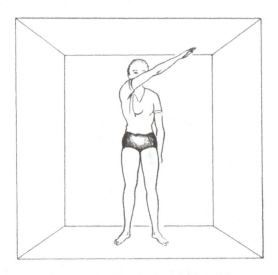

Figure 10: Taking your right arm across your body

Now reach as far as you can to the left, high back corner; carry on down towards the left, deep, back corner then along to left, deep, forward corner and up to your starting position. You will find that the pathway of the square you trace will undoubtedly be smaller than the one you made with your free left arm on that side, but keep the image of the four corners firmly fixed in your mind and reach towards them as far as you can, bending and arching your body while keeping your shoulders parallel with the front of the cube. Try, also, reversing the direction of the pathway.

### *Exploring the Right Side and Pathway (as in the first exercise) with the Left Arm*

● Repeat the instructions of the previous exercise, this time taking the left arm across the body to the right side. The most important thing is to have a clear understanding of where you are attempting to go even if you do not reach the final point.

### Exploring the Front Wall of the Cube with the Right Arm

● From stance, try a new pathway. Lift your right arm across your body to the left, high, forward corner of the cube, and move across to the right, high, forward corner. There is a feeling here of release, of opening out as the arm moves to its own side. Continue down to the right, deep corner with the same feeling. As you cross over to the left, deep corner and move up to the original starting position, the feeling of restriction will return. Now repeat the procedure with your left arm reaching across your body to the right, high, forward corner. This exercise demonstrates very clearly the restriction of movement when a limb is crossed to its opposite side, compared to the relative flexibility of movement on its own side. This will be further encountered in the Dimensional Scale.

### Exploring the Perimeter of the Back Wall of the Cube

● Exploring the perimeter of the back wall will represent a real challenge! Starting with your right arm (hand leading, of course) reach towards the right, high, back corner and move it down to the right, deep, back corner. Now move it across the deep, back edge to left, as far as it will go, allowing your body to twist to the right. Now what? Bring your hand away from the wall and let your arm do a detour across the front of your body and round it, turning as you go, until your hand can reach the point it has just left!

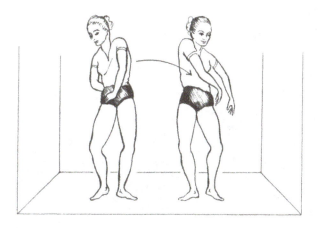

Figure 11: The detour round your body

Carry on along the deep, back edge to the corner and up the back, left edge to the top and finally, along the top, back edge to the starting position. The more reckless student could try going round the other way! Repeat the instructions of this exercise, this time leading with the left arm.

## Circling the Cube

It has been an important exercise to follow the direct pathways of the cube as precisely as possible. You will find that in circling around the cube, you are moving in a completely harmonious way with your bodily structure. The pathways will follow curves but still maintain the expressive qualities of high and deep, narrow and wide, backward and forward.

### Circling from Side to Side

● Take a slightly wider stance position with your feet. Transfer your weight to the right foot whilst simultaneously raising your right hand sideways to the centre of the right side of the cube. Keeping your arm out-stretched (elbow flexed), move it down past your feet (bent knees and body upright) to the left side, transferring your weight as you go. Continue the circle over your head, going onto the balls of your feet, until you return to the starting point with your weight back on your right foot.

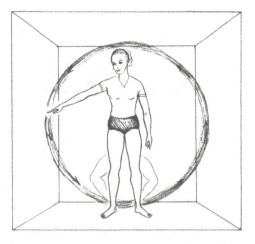

Figure 12: Circling the Cube from Side to Side

● Repeat the exercise several times before changing to the left side. Then try circling the other way round i.e. over high first.

### Circling from Front to Back

● Keeping the wider stance position, raise your left hand to the centre of the front wall of the cube. Circle down, bending your knees as you pass close to the outside of your left leg – this makes a slight deviation because your body blocks the path of the movement. Continue the circle behind you, rising onto the balls of your feet as your arm travels overhead to arrive once more at the starting position.

Figure 13: Circling from Front to Back

Try this several times, noting the bending and arching of the body. Try the right side several times, then try going the other way round, i.e. over high first.

### Circling Round your Waist

● Still keeping the wider stance, raise your right arm forward to the centre of the front wall of the cube and let your knees bend. Transferring your weight as you go, circle across to the left side and continue round, over the back, to make a complete circle with your hand at waist level, and your body following, to arrive once more at your starting position.

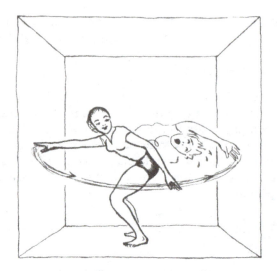

Figure 14: Circling Round your Waist

This is quite difficult, even for the experienced mover. It requires great flexibility of the trunk and will probably not be achieved successfully at first. Just keep trying! The aim is to keep the movement at waist level throughout.

● Repeat several times. Always aim for precision and try not to hold your breath. Shake out if you are stiffening up! Repeat this circle with the other side leading and then try both sides circling the other way round (i.e instead of moving over forward first, circle over backwards first).

## THE TETRAHEDRON

The tetrahedron is the smallest of the five crystals and is at the heart of the five polyhedra. Plato equated the tetrahedron with fire because it is the sharpest and most movable of the crystals. If we regard our dynamic movement of the body in a similar way, it is clear that the movement starts from the body centre, flowing out to the kinesphere.

If we agree that the crystals vibrate (and hasn't science shown us that atoms are full of movement?) it is in the tetrahedron that the smallest of vibrations occur. These are comparable to the small harmonic movements within ourselves which are barely visible such as our heart-beat and pulse and the miraculous, almost invisible breathing when we are asleep.

What are the particular qualities of movement within the tetrahedron? They require tension and they are expressive. Let us compare standing in an upright, flat, quadrangular position, which is relatively easy and requires very little tension and is certainly not very expressive, to a position exploring the three dimensions of the tetrahedron which will create considerable tension within the body.

Figure 15: Standing in an upright, flat, quadrangular position

In order to study this minute crystal, it is necessary to enlarge it until, when we stand inside it, our body centre corresponds to the centre of the tetrahedron. Almost all bodily positions can be linked to this shape. For our purposes we shall aim in three directions or at three vertices only, bearing in mind that the limb or part of the body that is supporting the weight is not counted as one of the directions as it is not part of the action.

Before you begin, picture clearly that the highest point is centred above your head and your feet are in the centre of the triangle on the floor. There is an option as to whether you face an edge or one of the three flat surfaces or planes. The following are five examples of positions in the tetrahedron where strong tension will be felt.

### Position 1

● From a comfortable kneeling position, facing an edge, extend your right foot into Point 1; extend your left hand to Point 2 and stretch your right arm high above your head so that your right hand is in the apex, Point 3. A strong tension between the three directions should be clearly felt. Your weight is on your left knee.

Figure 16: Position 1 in the Tetrahedron

## Position 2

- From a comfortable kneeling position, facing a plane, lift your right knee forward and lean forward so that nearly all of your weight is on your right foot; stretch your left foot into Point 1; take your right arm across your body down to Point 2 and stretch your left arm high above your head so that your left hand is in the apex, Point 3. Feel and note the tension.

Figure 17: Position 2 in the Tetrahedron

## Position 3

- From a comfortable position, standing in the middle of the base and facing an edge, take your weight on your left leg, letting it bend as you raise your right leg behind you as far as it will go towards the apex, Point 2. At the same time incline your body forwards and downwards as far as it will go, stretching your arms wide so that your hands reach Points 1 and 3. Note the considerable tension.

Figure 18: Position 3 in the Tetrahedron

## Position 4

For this position the tetrahedron is inverted and tilted slightly forward.

- From a comfortable standing position, step forward into the inverted apex with your left leg bending the knee and taking the weight. At the same time, raise your right leg behind you, pointing your foot into Point 1 and taking your right arm towards Point 2 (check that your left knee lies along the edge between Point 1 and the apex). Your head is at Point 3. Note the tension.

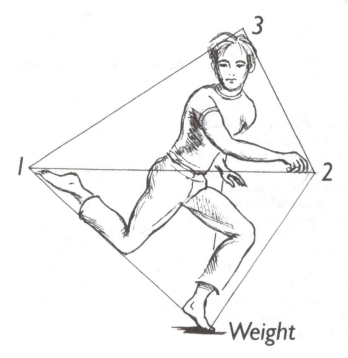

Figure 19: Position 4 in the Tetrahedron

## Position 5

For this position the tetrahedron is again standing on one of its points with a distinct backward lean.

- From a comfortable standing position, facing an edge, rise onto demi-point of your left foot with the knee bent; lift your right foot to Point 1 and stretch your left arm across your body to Point 2, at the same time curl your right arm around your head so that your elbow is in Point 3. Note the tension.

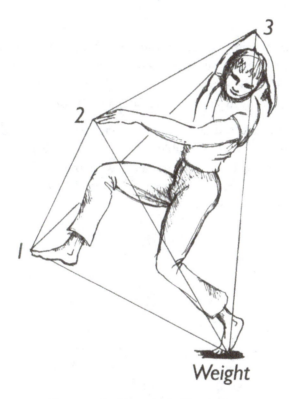

Figure 20: Position 5 in the Tetrahedron

All these positions can be reversed and, of course, you can try out ones of your own.

## THE OCTAHEDRON

The octahedron, being the second sharpest crystal after the tetrahedron, Plato assigned to air. It also has a relationship to the cube. If we were to encase a smaller octahedron inside a cube we would see that its six vertices correspond to the centres of the six planes of the cube.

As with the tetrahedron and cube, the octahedron must be sufficiently large in our mind for us to be able to move comfortably within it and for our body centre to be able to coincide with the centre of the crystal. Suppose you take stance in the imaginary octahedron, your feet placed on either side of the bottom point.

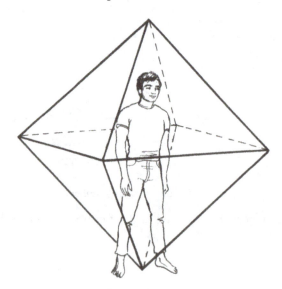

Figure 21: Stance position in the Octahedron

44

### *Exploring the Octahedron*

● With a clear picture of the shape in your mind, let your right hand explore the edges of each triangle in turn. There will be eight, of course, the back four being more difficult than the front. Following this, try the same exploration with your left hand.

### *An Octahedral 6-Ring*

The 6-ring, described below, is one of four belonging to the octahedron. It follows a circuitous route along the edges of the crystal, passing all the points or vertices and ending where it began. Hence the word, 'ring'. In this particular 6-ring, the 6 pathways are as follows: Right – High – Back – Left – Deep – Forward and back to Right.

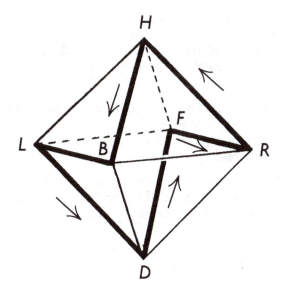

Figure 22: The Pathways of an Octahedral 6-Ring

● *Starting Position:* Turn yourself round to face point F and take a small half-step sideways to the right and reach out with your right hand to the right point (R), inclining your body in that direction.

● *Pathway 1.* Transfer your weight to your left foot and move your right foot forward a few inches and take your weight on it. Rise onto demi-pointe, simultaneously raising your left leg slightly off the ground as your right hand moves up the edge leading to the high point (H) above your head.

- *Pathway 2*. From H, your right hand travels along the edge leading to the back centre point B as you take a step backwards, briefly changing your weight onto your left foot and transferring it again onto your right foot, now positioned behind you. Your body should arch over backwards as far as it can to reach this centre back position. If it is too uncomfortable, turn the top half of your body sufficiently to the right to extend your right hand towards centre back.

- *Pathway 3*. From point B, the aim is to travel along the edge to L. You are already bending backwards and must keep doing so as you cross your right arm, closely over the front of your body to reach the left point (L), whilst simultaneously taking your weight briefly onto your left foot as your right foot crosses directly over to the left side and once more takes weight.

- *Pathway 4*. This requires transferring your weight briefly onto your left foot as you take your right foot back to stance position. With your weight evenly distributed on both your feet, bend your knees sufficiently for your right hand to travel from point L down to the floor at point D.

- *Pathway 5*. Rise to upright standing position, momentarily transferring your weight to your left foot whilst stepping forward onto your right foot, taking your weight as your right hand travels from point D up to point F.

- *Pathway 6*. Briefly take your weight onto your left foot and step to the right whilst your right hand travels from F to point R, bringing you back to your original starting position.

## THE DODECAHEDRON AND THE ICOSAHEDRON

The dodecahedron and the icosahedron are closely related. Just as the twelve surfaces or planes of the dodecahedron relate to the twelve points or vertices of the icosahedron, so do the twenty surfaces of the icosahedron relate to the twenty points of the smaller dodecahedron. Whereas the dodecahedron encourages smaller, inward movements, which relate to stability, the icosahedron encourages larger bodily movements reaching out into the kinesphere and beyond, often having a labile (or non-sustainable) quality. Because of this, Laban largely disregarded the dodecahedron from the movement point of view.

Laban believed that the icosahedron, the largest of the five crystals, was most closely related to the structure and movement ability of the human body. His idea of using it as the scaffolding of the kinesphere arose spontaneously from his study of movement and dance and his activity as a dancer and dance-teacher. Even so, he was astonished to find such a correspondence between the angles of the icosahedron and the maximum angles through which our limbs move. He also discovered that certain proportions within the icosahedron followed the law of the Golden Section. The Golden Section has long been connected with aesthetics but it was the Ancient Egyptians who first used it for their buildings and works of art. As far as we know, the Egyptians were purely instinctive in their use of the Golden Section; it was left to the Greeks to work out the mathematics of its proportion, and to Pythagoras who proved that the perfect human body is built according to its proportions.

**Note:** The Golden Section, since earliest times, has been universally recognised as a ratio or equation representating almost ideal proportions of balance and harmony. Not only were these proportions used in many ancient buildings such as the pyramids and the Parthenon, but they were found to be present in many forms of plant life (ferns in particular), animal life, and most significantly, the ideal human body. Leonardo da Vinci was later to demonstrate this in many of his paintings, and particularly in his drawing of the Vitruvian Man standing in a square and a circle.

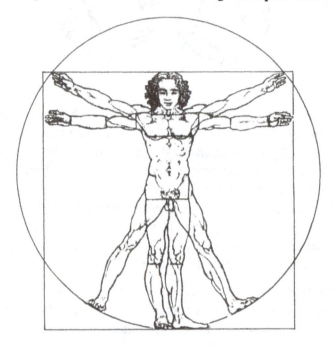

Figure 23: The Vitruvian Man (after Leonardo da Vinci)

And yet what is this Divine Ratio, this Divine Proportion? We are agog to know the answer, but the answer is disappointingly vague. To find the Golden Section, or the Golden Mean, we must divide a line from A to C at point B (very loosely at 3/8ths), so that the ratio of the large section, B to C, to the whole length, A to C, is the same ratio as the short section, A to B, is to B to C.

Point B is not very easy for us mere mortals to find. The experts will tell us that the Golden Ratio is approximately 1.62 or 1.618; a more accurate figure would be 1.6180339887498948482! But even this is an irrational number whose digits can carry on to infinity, telling us, perhaps, that the quest for absolute perfection can only be sought but never attained. A more tangible example of the Golden Section can be seen in the pentagram, where the intersection point of any two diagonals is at the Golden Section.

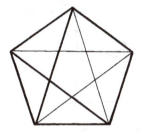

The properties of the Golden Rectangle – and you may as well be acquainted with this – are in accordance with the Golden Section, the short sides being 1. 618 etc. of the long sides. These rectangles are found in the icosahedron, three of which Laban used for the three Dimensional Planes.

## THE DIMENSIONAL CROSS
## AND THE THREE DIMENSIONAL PLANES

It is indicative of Laban's genius that he could see through all the complexities of human movement and simplify them into what he called the Dimensional Cross which is central to all his work.

The Dimensional Cross sounds like an object you can pick up. On the other hand, it sounds like a particular movement involving crossing. However, it is neither of these but is Laban's term for the spatial dimensions in which we move: upwards and downwards, backwards and forwards and from side to side. These three dimensions intersect at our body centre and are at the heart of our personal space or kinesphere. In the diagram (Figure 24) the Dimensional Cross is depicted as a vertical line, representing up and down, at the centre of which two horizontal lines cross at right angles, one representing from side to side, and the other representing backwards and forwards. In shape, being three-dimensional, it is similar to a weather-vane. It is customary to view such diagrams as though you are behind them, facing the same way, so the right and left sides correspond to yours. Using the dimensional terms, the Dimensional Cross looks like this:

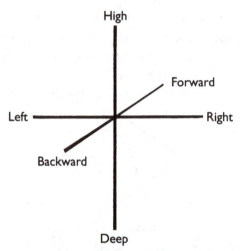

Figure 24: The Dimensional Cross with the Dimensional terms

However, when we use these three dimensions with our bodies and limbs, they become much wider than the rods of the diagram and evolve into three distinct planes: the High/Deep dimension extends to right and left and becomes what Laban called the Door Plane; the Forward/Backward dimension extends high and deep and becomes what Laban called the Wheel Plane; the Right/Left dimension extends forwards and backwards and becomes what Laban called the Table Plane. Fitted together as a geometrical construction they look like this:

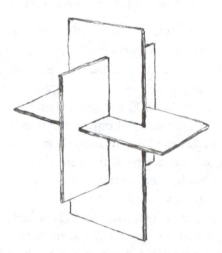

Figure 25: The Three Dimensional Planes

What is truly remarkable is that these three planes or rectangles can be clearly detected within the icosahedron, their twelve corners corresponding with the twelve points. To observe this, the icosahedron should be viewed standing not on one of its faces but balanced on one of its edges, the viewer standing slightly to the right of it.

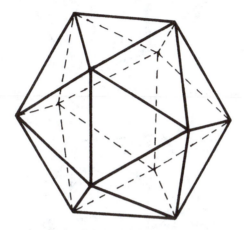

Figure 26: The Icosahedron, poised on one of its edges viewed, slightly from the right

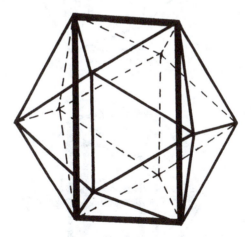

Figure 27: The Icosahedron showing the Door Plane

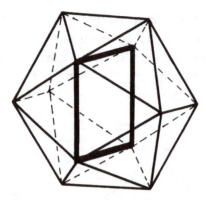

Figure 28: The Icosahedron showing the Wheel Plane

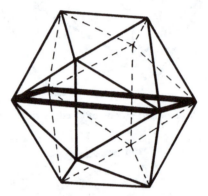

Figure 29: The Icosahedron showing the Table Plane

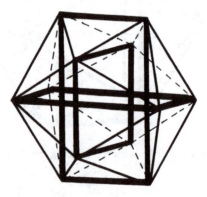

Figure 30: The Icosahedron showing all three Planes

### Experiencing the Door Plane

● To experience the Door Plane, stand with your feet rather more
than a shoulder-width apart and stretch your arms above your
head, similarly apart. You should feel very wall-like and flat.
The Door Plane is so-called because it is very like standing in a
doorway with your feet and hands reaching into its four corners.
In this position you are dividing the space around you into two
halves – that which is behind you and that which is in front of you.
There is an upward-downward stress to this plane.

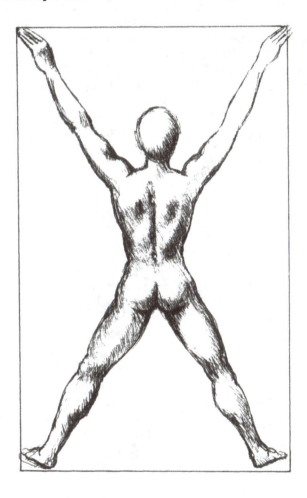

Figure 31: Standing in the Door Plane

### *Experiencing the Wheel Plane*

● In spite of its rectangular shape, the Forward/Backward dimension is commonly called the Wheel Plane, presumably because there is a greater feeling of rotation than in the other planes. To experience the Wheel Plane, take a stride forward with your left foot and transfer your weight onto it. Stretch your right arm forward to the higher point of the wheel plane rectangle, approximately at eye level with your hand positioned directly in front of your nose. Then move your right arm to the lower point (immediately underneath it), approximately at knee level. Now, transfer your weight to your right leg in the backward position, and move your right arm as though through your body to the same level directly behind you, while bringing your left arm forward to the higher point, simultaneously lowering your left arm. Finally, bring your right arm up behind you to a point behind your head and level with the first point. With the Wheel Plane you are again dividing the space into two halves, that which is on the left side of your body and that which is on the right. There is a forward/backward stress to this plane.

Figure 32: Standing in the Wheel Plane

## *Experiencing the Table Plane*

● To experience the Table Plane, imagine you are standing in the middle of a rectangular table which fits comfortably around your waist. Feel the flatness all round you with your hands and then feel the four corners. The Table Plane stresses the sideways dimension. To reach the front corners you will have to lean forward whilst your arms stretch outwards and forwards; to reach the back corners you will have to arch backward whilst your arms stretch outwards and backwards. With the Table Plane you are again dividing the space around you into two halves, that which is above your waist and that which is below. There is a side-to-side stress to this plane.

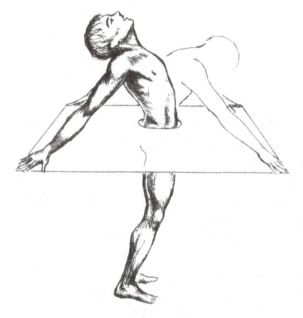

Figure 33: Standing in the Table Plane

Having described the individual characteristics of each of the three planes, it should be pointed out that they have an affinity to each other. We have noted that the strongest influence of the Door Plane is its upward/downward stress. However, the two shorter parallel edges at the top and bottom of the rectangle reach out sideways which therefore gives it an affinity to the Table Plane. The strongest influence of the Table Plane is its sideways stress. Here, the two shorter parallel sides of the rectangle reach towards the forward and backward dimension which therefore gives it an affinity to the Wheel Plane. The strongest influence in the Wheel Plane is the forward/backward stress. Its shorter parallel sides of the rectangle also reach upwards/downwards giving it an affinity to the Door Plane.

We can deduce from this that dimensions have their own qualities of expression. When they become Planes, whilst maintaining these individual qualities, the secondary influence is clearly noticeable.

The 3 Planes provide the icosahedron with 12 points of spatial reference. They also provide a network of inter-related points, planes and transversals, as well as dividing our personal space into areas, opening up still further networks.

## LEVELS AND ZONES

### Levels

Laban believed there were three 'types' of dancers (or movers generally). Those who enjoy moving in the high level, such as leaping and springing off the ground. Those who enjoy moving in the central level, their bodies leading with more sensuous movements. And those who enjoy moving in the deep level (often strongly built), who prefer more earth-bound movements. He also believed that people could, with training, extend their movement range, ideally, being able to leap, move sensuously and to show strength, particularly in the legs. This is very different from the classical ballet dancer image, whose physique must conform to certain rules, and they are rarely, if ever, required to perform strong, earth-bound movements in the deep level.

### Zones

If you stand upright with your feet well apart and your arms stretched outwards (see Figure 31), it is very clear, from this position, that your head moves naturally in the high zone, the arms and hands move naturally in the middle to higher zone and the legs and feet move naturally in the deep zone. The limbs have their own natural area or zone but can cross to their opposite side. If you imagine yourself standing in a pentagon, and remembering that the intersection of any two diagonals is at a Golden Section, Figure 34 will show you not only the zones but also the body's proportions in relation to the Golden Section.

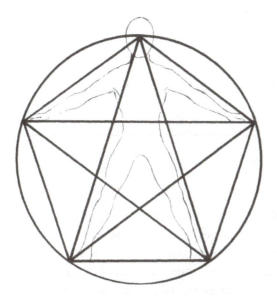

Figure 34: A flat, pentagonal pose of the body showing the Zones (after Laban)

There is nothing strange about asking you to raise your arms above your head but if you were asked to raise your foot above your head you would think it beyond the bounds of possibility unless you were double-jointed or incredibly supple. Even so, your foot would be required to enter a strange zone. It would certainly be unusual for people in everyday life, including actors. Not so, for most dancers, but Laban was determined that less able movers, who had little movement training, should still experience the feeling of legs reaching above the head, moving in the high zone. Students were required to move around on the floor, with their legs performing various patterns in the air! Many of these early improvised activities were seen as a joke at first. But the students soon realised that, apart from increasing their mobility, it gave them a new perspective; actors, in particular, enjoyed the experience, sometimes calling on it to assist in their improvisations. Try it yourself. Lie on the floor and see how high you can reach with your feet towards the ceiling. Then try reaching obliquely towards the corners of the room. This exercise is valuable for increasing mobility, especially in the legs, because they can move without carrying body weight.

## ARCS AND CIRCLES

The ancient Greek word *choreo-sophia* (choreo-sophy) meant the knowledge or wisdom of circles which were believed to have magical powers. (Choreo meaning dance, especially choral dance with music, and of any circling motion as of the stars.) Indeed, in early Greece, at the dithyrambic contests, the *choreutae* of a tribe would march in, in single file to the orchestra, and immediately form a circle around the altar. As they began their song, they would move, sometimes to the right, sometimes to the left, whilst at other times they remained standing still. The ritual circle dance, whether in the form of a stately procession or arranged with dance-like steps, was probably the commonest kind of sacred dance. Throughout the centuries, the circle dance spread world-wide and the object at the heart of the circle around which the dancers moved was sacred, a sacrificial victim, a well, a holy tree or an altar. The dithyrambic dance circled the altar of Dionysus; Plato's name was linked to the 'emmeleia' or peace dance, often associated with the highest form of Greek tragedy.

Deemed to be endowed with mystical properties, the circle dances continued to feature in religious ceremonies and social rites down the ages. Their unifying presence in everyday life was considered vital for promoting an harmonious existence.

The earth makes a circle round the sun at a regular interval which has been subdivided into what we know as twenty-four hours. Its pathway is linked to other heavenly bodies which also move regularly around their own orbital pathways. This observation of the heavenly bodies has given rise to a sense of order and of Time. The sun was our time-keeper which defined night and day. Plato believed that we were all endlessly reborn, the soul leaving the natural world and being reborn into it like a spiral reaching upwards to perfection. It is a sobering thought that the soul could also spiral downwards! The whole of Plato's world was circular, the zodiac, the cycle of life and death, the returning and the renewing. In this context, the circle has a logic about it which is easy to follow. Movement is at the heart of life itself and man is a natural part of this world.

Even today, tribes have their circle dances for invoking the gods, whether for rain, fertility or success at hunting. Apart from many folk dances throughout Europe being circular in their formation, groups of circle dancers meet to practise their dances, usually dancing round a candle, believing the circle and the communion with each other to have a healing process.

1. **Choreo-graphy,** or the writing of circles, which today is interpreted more widely as the creation of dances. A choreo-grapher is a composer or creator of dances, and differs from a dance teacher in that he or she devises a complete dance or series of dances into a composite whole with a view to presenting it as a spectacle to an audience. Nor is the choreo-grapher confined to dance, but is often called upon to devise movement sequences and even fights in stage productions.

2. **Choreo-logy** is the logic or science of the circles which might be considered as pure **geometry** which, though a branch of mathematics, has much deeper implications. **Geometrics** does not deal solely with the outer visible form of movement but also the mental and emotional content. There isn't a good word in English to indicate the coming together of the physical, mental and emotional content, but in German it is called a *gestalt.*

3. **Chore-utics** simply means the practical study of the various forms of movement. The harmonious influence of circles was mentioned earlier and **chore-utics** also contains this harmonic element. Today, the word **choreutics** has been superceded by the study of 'spatial harmony' which

is preferable and allows for the fact that not all things in life are harmonious. It should be remembered that harmony encompasses discord as well as concord and this is reflected in everything around us. Witness the deformities in nature. An ancient gnarled tree has a beauty of its own; a person with a slight limp can seem dignified and impressive; a crumbling building or a ruin is usually more picturesque than a brand new edifice. In music, it is the discords that make harmony interesting, because they create more tension. Constant concords can quickly pall on the ear.

As far as human movement is concerned, every movement we make creates an arc or a circle. If we move a finger, it moves in an arc or a circle because one end is fixed to the hand; likewise, the hand moves in arcs and circles because it is fixed to the wrist; the forearm moves in arcs and circles because it is attached to the elbow and the upper arm, likewise because it is fixed to the shoulder. The same applies to our feet (toes are difficult), lower legs and full legs – when we swing a leg or whole arm, it makes a large curve. Our hips move in circles, so do our shoulders; if we bend from side to side or backwards and forwards we create an arc. Our heads can only move in arcs and circles. In short, it is impossible to move any part of ourselves in a straight line.

## NOTATION

Before we embark on the Dimensional and other Scales, it is a good idea to introduce some basic symbols of notation which can assist in a clearer understanding of the height and direction of movements and in due course should help you to be able to jot your own movements down.

Ever since he committed his life to dance and movement, Laban searched endlessly for a method of writing down dance movements and, indeed, every other form of movement. He studied the earlier attempts of Arbeau, Rameau, Feuillet and the great French eighteenth-century ballet-master, Jean Georges Noverre, and found them all inadequate – they could do little more than notate steps and floor patterns. Laban, however, was convinced that a notation system could be devised that would cover every articulation of the human physique and that would also indicate the expressive nature of these movements. In between all his other multifarious activities, he laboured on and off over many years to find the ideal system and, having started it, he handed it over to Albrecht Knust who devoted his life to polishing and perfecting what is now known as Labanotation. These three notation symbols indicate the levels in space:-

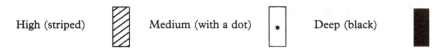

High (striped)     Medium (with a dot)     Deep (black)

The following symbols indicate both the levels and the directions of movements.

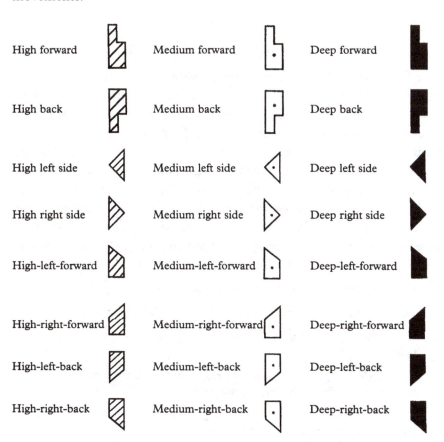

High forward     Medium forward     Deep forward

High back     Medium back     Deep back

High left side     Medium left side     Deep left side

High right side     Medium right side     Deep right side

High-left-forward     Medium-left-forward     Deep-left-forward

High-right-forward     Medium-right-forward     Deep-right-forward

High-left-back     Medium-left-back     Deep-left-back

High-right-back     Medium-right-back     Deep-right-back

We shall be using notation later.

# 2

# *The Movement Scales*

Laban devised many movement scales but it is sufficient for us to concentrate on five of them; the Dimensional Scale, the Diagonal Scale, the 'A' Scale, the 'B' Scale and the Primary Scale.

## THE DIMENSIONAL SCALE

The Dimensional Scale is looked upon as the 'stable' scale. This means that it is relatively easy to maintain balance as the body moves between a vertical or horizontal position whilst supported on one leg. It is also known as the Defence Scale because its six positions are based on those used to defend the six most vulnerable areas of the body and head. According to whether the defender is left-handed or right-handed, he will hold his weapon in the 'strong' hand. If this were wounded and the weapon were held in the 'weaker' hand, his chances of survival could be seriously jeopardised. Defence of the body depends on anatomical structure and the ability of the body and limbs to move well in their zones. Assuming that the defender is right-handed, he will:

1. Raise his right arm upwards to protect his face.

2. Lower the right arm downwards to protect his right side (flank).

3. Cross the right arm over to the left to protect his left jugular vein.

4. Take the right arm across to the right to deflect the attacker's weapon away from the right jugular vein.

5. His right arm will move across his body backwards, to guard the left flank from the attacker's weapon.

6. His abdomen is shielded by a forward movement repulsing the attacker.

The left-handed defender will, of course, lead with his left hand. The right and left sideways dimension of the Dimensional Scale is linked to the Space continuum. This means that the right arm (or leg) is able to move flexibly on its own right side but crossing to the left it produces a movement that is not so flexible and therefore more direct. The reverse is true for the left side. Remember that the numbering refers to the preceding movement pathway as well as to its ultimate 'point' or position.

**The Dimensional Scale for the Right Side**

● *Pathway 1:* From stance, take a very small step forward with your right foot on demi-pointe, placing your entire weight on it. Simultaneously, stretch your right arm upwards until it is in the High dimension. Your left arm and leg should be directly behind in Deep counter-tension.

● *Pathway 2:* From (1), release the weight from your forward foot, bringing it slightly backwards to a new position just behind your left foot where it will again take weight. Simultaneously, lower your right arm so that your whole body takes an upright, semi-squatting position whilst the 'heel' of your hand presses down by your right side. Your left hand also presses down whilst your body is stretching upward in counter-tension. Return to the stance position. Try (1) and (2) several times.

● *Pathway 3:* Rising from (2), step over to your
left side with your right foot crossing in front
of your left foot. At the same time, bring your
right arm across your body to the left sideways
dimension (3), with your thumb leading and
the back of your hand brushing against your
chest. Bend your left arm in a close horizontal
position behind you, brushing your back in
counter-tension. In order to prevent your body
also turning to the left, turn your right foot out
so that your right heel leads the movement.
(It helps also to keep your right hip back.)
Your weight is on your right leg, with your
knees bent and as close together as possible
with both feet out-turned. The feeling is one
of sideways balance.

The whole position may feel a little awkward but try and keep your body
vertical even when your knees are bent. The feeling is one of narrowness
and flatness; consequently, in this extremely restricted space, the movement pathway is confined to a direct approach.

● *Pathway 4:* From this narrow, flat side, move your right leg to the
right in a wide stride, taking the full weight of your body on your
out-turned right foot. As you extend your right arm outwards,
reach out horizontally as far as you can with your left arm and leg
in counter-tension to it. The quality of expression is one of 'width'
and spatial freedom. This is very different from the narrowness of
the crossed side, although it still maintains the sideways dimensional flat quality. Repeat (3) and (4) several times.

- *Pathway 5:* From this out-stretched position, return fleetingly through stance and let your right heel brush your left before it steps into the Backwards dimension and takes weight again (5). We now encounter a problem. If you take your right arm backwards over your right side, your body will want to turn to follow which would take you into the sideways dimension. To overcome this, bring your right arm across your body and under your left armpit. This provides greater tension and helps your body maintain its 'front' while it arches backwards, strongly counter-balancing your left leg and left arm which are raised horizontally in front.

- *Pathway 6:* Briefly return to stance and step forward with your right foot and take your weight on it completely, lifting your left leg into a horizontal position behind you. At the same time, stretch your right arm forwards and your left arm backwards in strong counter-tension. Repeat (5) and (6) several times before trying the whole scale through without the repetitions.

### The Flowing Version for the Right Side

When you have perfected each of the six pathways, you can then experience the sheer pleasure of moving through these pathways in a flowing and harmonious way. This is where the scale becomes dance. For the Flowing Version, try the scale following curved pathways instead of going straight from point to point. At first, taking it in three pairs i.e. (1) and (2), next (3) and (4) and finally, (5) and (6). Each pair should flow smoothly in a series of 'figure eights' where the counter-tension will be felt. The weight should transfer from foot to foot in repetition.

● *Dimension 1-2.* Take a small half-step forward with your right foot and put weight on it as you swing your right arm from Medium level over left to High and return to body centre over the right side to Medium level again. This is your first loop of a figure eight. Now take a small half-step backward, again making the figure eight, as you continue swinging your right arm, crossing behind your body to centre deep. Bend your knees as you go before rising and returning to the right side at Medium level, thus completing the second loop of a figure eight. This can be repeated harmoniously many times.

- *Dimension 3-4.* Cross your right foot over to the left side which takes weight as your right arm swings to the left through Medium-low and back through Medium-high (first loop). Transferring your weight to your right foot as you step to the right, your arm moves across to the right side through Medium-low and returns through Medium-high. This is your second loop. This can be repeated harmoniously many times.

- *Dimension 5-6.* Your feet should be more apart than in the first dimensional position. Put weight on your right foot as you step backwards whilst your right arm swings over backwards on the left side, Medium-low and returns over Medium-high to body centre, thus forming the first loop. (Your left arm is raised a little to allow the right arm to move backwards freely). The movement continues as you step forward on your right foot taking weight on it, as the right arm now swings over Medium-low Forward, returning over Medium-high Backward to body centre. This is your second loop. This can be repeated harmoniously many times. When you have

perfected each of these pairs, join them all together to make one continuous, flowing movement.

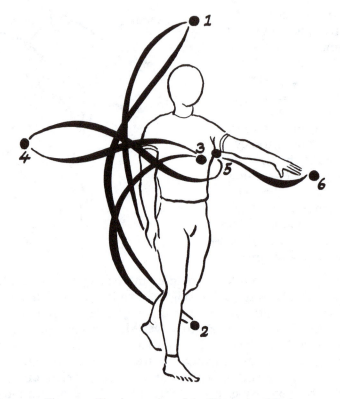

Figure 35: Flowing version of the Dimensional Scale

## The Dimensional Scale for the Left Side

- *Pathway 1:* Take a very small step forward with the left foot, on demi-pointe, placing your entire weight on it. Simultaneously, stretch your left arm upwards until it is in the High dimension, your left foot still on the demi-pointe. Your right arm and leg should be directly behind in Deep counter-tension.

- *Pathway 2:* from (1), release the weight from your forward foot, bringing it slightly backwards to a new position just behind your right foot where it will again take weight. Simultaneously, lower your left arm and your whole body which takes an upright, semi-squatting position whilst the 'heel' of your hand presses down by your left side. Your right hand also presses down whilst your body is in counter-tension, striving to High. Return to the stance position. Try (1) and (2) several times.

- *Pathway 3:* Your left arm and leg are now going to move horizontally across your body to the right sideways dimension (3). In order to prevent your body turning to face the direction to which you are travelling, turn your left foot out so that your left heel leads the movement. (It helps also to keep your left hip back.) The weight is on the left leg, with your knees bent and as close together as possible. Your feet should be out-turned. The feeling is one of sideways balance. Meanwhile, your left arm has travelled across your chest with your thumb leading and the back of your hand brushing your chest, taking it no further than the right side of your chest. Your right arm is bent in a close position behind you, brushing your back in counter-tension.

- *Pathway 4:* From this narrow, flat side, move your left leg to the left in a wide stride and take the full weight of your body on your out-turned left foot. As you extend your left arm outwards, reach out horizontally as far as you can with your right arm and leg in counter-tension to it. Repeat (3) and (4) several times.

- *Pathway 5:* From this out-stretched position, return fleetingly through stance and let your left heel brush your right before it steps into the Backwards dimension and takes weight again (5). To prevent your body from turning to the left, bring your left arm across your body and under your right armpit. This provides greater tension and helps your body maintain its 'front' while it arches backwards, strongly counter-balancing your right leg and right arm which are raised horizontally in front.

- *Pathway 6:* Briefly return to stance and step forward with your left foot and take your weight on it completely, lifting your right leg into a horizontal position behind you. At the same time, stretch your left arm forwards and your right arm backwards in strong counter-tension. Repeat (5) and (6) several times before trying the whole scale through without the repetitions. Try to keep facing front and this will greatly assist your moves into the six pathways.

### The Flowing Version for the Left Side

● As before, for the Flowing Version, try the scale following curved pathways, at first taking it in three pairs i.e. (1) and (2), next (3) and (4) and finally, (5) and (6). Each pair should flow smoothly in a series of 'figure eights' where the counter-tension will be felt. Remember to transfer your weight from foot to foot in repetition. When you have perfected each of these pairs, join them all together in one continuous movement.

### The Three Crosses:
### the Dimensional, the Diametral and the Diagonal

The **Dimensional Cross**, as we have just seen from the Dimensional Scale, moves in six directions: directly to High or Deep, Right or Left, Backward or Forward. This is the basis of our spatial 'map' and what is referred to as the **given norm**. Any other direction being a deflection

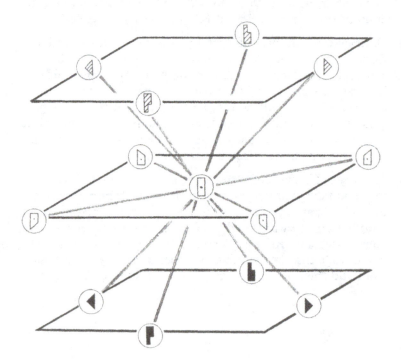

Figure 36: The six-diametral cross

from the given norm. The **Diametral Cross** moves in six diameters: Right High to Left Deep; Left High to Right Deep; Forward High to Backward Deep; Backward High to Forward Deep; Left Backward to Right Forward; Right Backward to Left Forward, all of which are deflections from the given norm. Each of these six diameters can start from the opposite end, making 12 deflected directions in all.

The **Diagonal Cross** moves in three directions, simultaneously: Right/High/Forward to Left/Deep/Backward; Left/High/Forward to Right/Deep/Backward; Left/High/Backward to Right/Deep/Forward; Right/High/Backward to Left/Deep/Forward, making four pathways. These directions can be reversed making a total of eight pathways. All the directions or pathways of these three crosses intersect at the centre of the body.

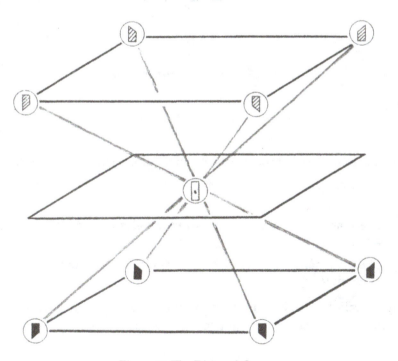

Figure 37: The Diagonal Cross

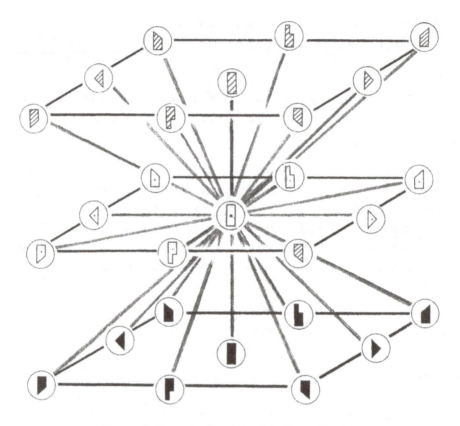

Figure 38: The main directions of the Three Crosses

The diagram above shows the three levels of the cube and its link with:

A   The dimensional cross, the given norm, moving in one direction only.

B   The diametral cross, deflected from the given norm, moving in two dimensions.

C   The diagonal cross, also deflected from the given norm, moves in three directions.

The directions can, of course, be innumerable, radiating from the body centre through the kinesphere and beyond into infinite space.

## THE DIAGONAL SCALE

As we have seen, the Dimensional Scale moves in one dimensional direction at a time and it has a stabilising effect on the body; positions can be held. In the Diagonal Scale, no position can be held because it is so fleeting and every point reached finds the body at its most unstable. Laban preferred the expression *labile* as an alternative to unstable and, therefore, this scale was said to have a *labile* quality. This makes it harder to do in slow motion which is necessary when you are learning it. Moving into three dimensions simultaneously, the mover, momentarily, is off-balance before the pull of gravity swiftly intervenes and returns the mover to a more 'realistic' stability.

Remember that the diagonals, as in all movement scales, continue beyond your reach. Let us go through the pathway of each diagonal slowly before you attempt springing off the ground. Each diagonal will be explored separately before returning to stance. Later, the scale will be worked through as a series of continuous swinging pathways with no interruptions. Do not face the diagonal corner you are moving into but make sure it is always to your right or left side.

### The Diagonal Scale for the Right Side

It is helpful to imagine yourself once again in the centre of the cube. The numbers refer to the sequential order.

● *Pathway 1:* From stance, take a step to Right/Forward and immediately spring towards the Right/High/Forward diagonal (1), stretching your right arm and inclining your body in the same direction. Your left arm and leg should be behind in counter-tension. Return to stance.

- *Pathway 2:* After the spring, step briefly back on your left foot then take your right leg behind your left, to Left/Deep/Back (2), and kneel on it. This is the same diagonal in reverse order to Pathway 1. Your right arm should simultaneously cross in front of your chest to stretch in the same direction of Left/Deep/Back (2). You will find that your body arches and inclines over left to assist the movement. Your left arm should be in counter-tension in the direction of Right/High/Forward (1). Return to stance.

- *Pathway 3:* Take a crossing step towards the point Left/High/Forward (3), springing as you stretch your right arm and incline your body in the same direction. (Try to keep facing directly forward.) Your left leg (with flexed knee) and left arm are pointing to the opposite end of this same diagonal Right/Deep/Back (4). Your left knee should be sufficiently across your body for you to look over your right shoulder and see your left foot. Return to stance.

● *Pathway 4:* This is the same diagonal in reverse order as Pathway 3, arriving at Right/Deep/Back (4) from Left/High/Forward (3). On landing from the spring, move your right leg to point Right/Deep/Back (4), taking your weight and bending the knee. Simultaneously, your right arm travels in the same open direction and points towards Right/Deep/Back (4). In counter-tension, your left arm and leg are raised in the direction of point Left/High/Forward (3). Return to stance.

● *Pathway 5:* Step across and behind your left leg, springing in the direction of point Left/High/Back (5), whilst your right arm stretches across your inclined body (about shoulder level) into the same direction Left/High/Back (5). Your left arm and leg cross in counter-tension to this diagonal's opposite end Right/Deep/Forward (6). Try to keep facing forward. Return to stance.

● *Pathway 6:* This is the same diagonal in reverse order as Pathway 5. Step briefly onto your left foot and spring low onto your right leg to Right/Deep/Forward (6), bending your knee and stretching your right arm in the same direction. Meanwhile, your left arm and leg should be behind in counter-tension at point Left/High/Back (5). Return to stance.

● *Pathway 7:* Step back briefly onto your left foot and follow with a spring to the point Right/High/Back (7), simultaneously stretching your right arm in the same direction. Your left arm and leg should point to the reverse end of the same diagonal Left/Deep/Forward (8) in counter-tension. Return to stance.

● *Pathway 8:* This diagonal is in reverse order, arriving at point Left/Deep/Forward (8) from Right/High/Back (7). This final diagonal of the scale brings your right leg (knee bent) across to point Left/Deep/Forward (8) with a low spring as your right arm also stretches to the same point. Try to keep facing forward whilst your left arm and leg are in counter-tension (Right/High/Back), your left leg sufficiently crossed behind your body to enable you to look over your right shoulder to see your left foot.

Each diagonal position has ended in stance for clarification and a breathing space. Now you must consider the transitions linking one end of a diagonal to the next in sequence. They are worth studying separately. For instance, taking up a starting position in (2) and moving along a pathway to (3), you will find all your limbs are moved from one closed position to another. From a starting position in (4) and moving along a pathway to (5), you are leaving an open position and moving to a closed position. From position (6) to (7), you move from one open side to another. To repeat the scale, moving from (8) to (1), will mean leaving a closed position and moving into an open position.

## The Flowing Version for the Right Side

Now go through the diagonals without the breaks, omitting stance. For example, after swinging up to point (1) in a harmoniously curving manner and then down to its opposite end point Left/Deep/Back (2) (do not kneel in this instance but bend the right knee as fully as possible), rise and swing in another curving pathway and immediately spring into diagonal point Left/High/Forward (3). You will find your body will naturally tilt to follow the leading arm even though your front remains constant. Continue through the scale, trying it several times until it has a swinging 'lilt' to it.

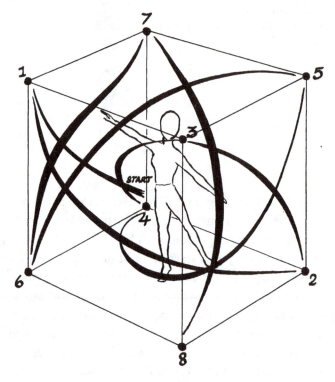

Figure 39: Flowing version of the Diagonal Scale

It is possible to try the whole exercise starting at the opposite ends of the diagonals. For example, try starting in point (R/H/F) and moving to (L/D/B), (R/H/F), (R/D/B), (L/H/F) to (R/D/B), (R/F/D) to (L/B/H), and (R/H/B) to (L/D/F). After a breathing space, you are ready to do the scale with the left side leading.

## The Diagonal Scale for The Left Side.

Imagine yourself once again in the centre of the cube.

- *Pathway 1:* From stance, take a step Left/Forward and immediately spring towards the Left/High/Forward diagonal (1), stretching your left arm and inclining your body in the same direction. Your right arm and leg should be stretched behind in counter-tension. Return to stance.

- *Pathway 2:* This is the same diagonal in reverse order, arriving at point Right/Deep/Back (2) from point Left/High/Forward (1). After the spring, step briefly back on your right foot then take your left leg behind your right to Right/Deep/Back (2) and kneel on it. Your left arm should simultaneously cross in front of your chest to stretch in the same direction of Right/Deep/Back (2). You will find that your body arches and inclines over right to assist the movement. Your right arm and leg in should be in counter-tension in the direction of Left/High/Forward (1). Return to stance.

- *Pathway 3:* Take a crossing step towards the point Right/High/Forward (3), springing as you stretch your left arm and incline your body in the same direction. (Try to keep facing directly forward.) Your right leg (with slightly flexed knee) and right arm are pointing to the opposite end of this same diagonal Left/Deep/Back (4). Your right knee should be sufficiently across your body for you to look over your left shoulder and see your right foot. Return to stance.

- *Pathway 4:* This is the same diagonal in reverse order, arriving at Left/Deep/Back (4) from Right/High/Forward (3). On landing from the spring, your left leg moves to point Left/Deep/Back(4) and takes weight. Your left knee is bent. Simultaneously, the left arm travels in the same open direction and points towards Left/Deep/Back (4). In counter-tension, your right arm and leg are raised in the direction of point Right/High/Forward (3). Return to stance.

- *Pathway 5:* Step across and behind your right leg, springing in the direction of point Right/High/Back (5), whilst your left arm stretches across your inclined body (about shoulder level) into the same direction Right/High/Back (5). Your right arm and leg cross in counter-tension to this diagonal's opposite end Left/Deep/Forward (6). Try to keep facing forward. Return to stance.

- Pathway 6: This is the same diagonal in reverse order to Pathway 5. Step briefly onto your right foot and spring low onto your left leg to Left/Deep/Forward (6), bending the knee and stretching your left arm in the same direction. Meanwhile, your right arm and leg should be behind in counter-tension at point Right/High/Back (5). Return to stance.

- Pathway 7: Step back briefly onto your right foot and follow with a spring to the point Left/High/Back (7), simultaneously stretching your right arm in the same direction. Your right arm and leg should point to the reverse end of the same diagonal Right/Deep/Forward (8) in counter-tension. Return to stance.

- Pathway 8: This final diagonal of the scale brings your left leg (knee bent) across to point Right/Deep/Forward (8) with a low spring as your left arm also stretches to the same point. Try to keep facing forward whilst your right arm and leg are in counter-tension (Left/High/Back), your right leg sufficiently crossed behind your body to enable you to look over your left shoulder to see your right foot.

## The Flowing Version for the Left Side

- Now go through the diagonals without the breaks, omitting stance. As before, after swinging up to point (1) in a harmoniously curving manner and then down to its opposite end point Right/Deep/Back (2) (remember not to kneel in this instance but bend your left knee as fully as possible) rise and swing in another curving pathway and immediately spring into diagonal point Right/High/Forward (3). You will find your body will naturally tilt to follow the leading arm even though your front remains constant. Continue through the scale, trying it several times until it has a swinging 'lilt' to it, combining the natural arcs and curves of the body with the harmonious pathways of the diagonals.

Again, it is possible to try the whole exercise starting at the opposite ends of the diagonals.

- Try starting in point (2) and moving to (1); (4) to (3); (6) to (5); and (8) to (7). The cube's diagonals coincide with those relating to the body's kinesphere, intersecting at the body's centre.

## THE 'A' SCALE

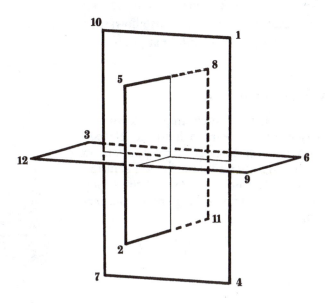

Figure 40: The Three Planes showing the 12 signal points as for the right side

The 'A' Scale is comprised of transversals connecting the twelve signal points or vertices of the three Planes which form an integral part of the 'scaffolding' of the icosahedron. They are movement pathways which traverse the icosahedron without passing through its centre (or through the body centre) linking two vertices. Each transversal has its parallel. The pathways of the transversals differ from the pathways of the dimensional, diametric and diagonal crosses which all intersect at body centre and the centre of your kinesphere, in that they have a steep, flat or flowing stress according to the plane from which they originate. Laban considered the 'A' Scale to be in the minor key in contrast to the major key of the 'B' Scale.

When following the pathways of the scales, it is important to remind ourselves that the numbering actually relates to the pathway immediately preceding the point as well as to the arrival point. One side of the body will be leading the movement into each new spatial direction whilst the opposite foot remains close to stance momentarily taking weight as the body moves into each new direction. It will then move into counter-tension.

The first six movements of the 'A' Scale bear a relationship to the Dimensional or Defence Scale and our starting position will be the last point of the scale i.e. Point 12. This allows us to move along the whole length of the first pathway ending at point 1.

### The 'A' Scale for the Right Side

● *Preparation:* From stance, step back with your right foot crossing behind the left leg to the Left/Deep/Back corner. Simultaneously, take your right hand under the left arm to reach towards point Left/Back of the Table Plane. Your left arm and leg are in counter-tension.

● *Pathway 1:* From Left/Back, your right arm moves to point Right/High (1) of the Door Plane. Your right foot steps to the right taking weight; the heel is slightly raised off the floor but is not completely balanced on the ball of your foot or demi-pointe. Meanwhile your left side is in counter-tension. The movement from (12) to (1) has a flat stress owing to its originating from the Table Plane.

82

- *Pathway 2:* From
  Right/High, the pathway
  moves your right arm and
  leg to point Deep/Back
  (2) of the Wheel Plane.
  The Deep/Back position
  lifts your left leg in its
  forward countertension
  position. This movement
  from (1) to (2) has a steep
  stress as it originates from
  the Door Plane.

- *Pathway 3:* From Deep/Back your right arm and
  leg cross over to the left side in front, your arm
  moving into point Left/Forward (3) of the Table
  Plane. Try to keep facing front.
  Your body is almost horizontal
  at this medium level. Your left
  leg (knee slightly bent) is
  sufficiently inclined to the right side
  in counter-tension for you to look over
  your right shoulder at the left foot. This
  movement from (2) to (3) has a 'flowing'
  stress as it originates from the Wheel Plane. The
  sequence of flat, steep and flowing continues
  in rotation thoughout the scale.

- *Pathway 4:* Your movement takes you to point Right/Deep (4) of the Door Plane. Your right leg is in a deep bend, your right arm reaches to point (4). Your left leg is outstretched, the foot touching the ground and the arm raised in counter-tension. This movement from (3) to (4) has a flat stress as it originates from the Table Plane.

- *Pathway 5:* Your right leg steps centre back as your right arm moves to point High/Back (5). The counter-tension is Deep/Forward. This movement from (4) to (5) has a steep stress as it originates from the Door Plane.

84

● *Pathway 6:* Your right arm is going to move to Right/Forward (6) as your right leg steps in the same direction. At medium level, your body can attempt to take up a horizontal position, lifting your left leg and arm backwards in counter-tension. This movement from (5) to (6) has a flowing stress as it originates from the Wheel Plane.

● *Pathway 7:* Your right arm and leg are going to move across, in front of your body, to point Left/Deep (7). Your right knee is bent and takes the weight whilst your right arm crosses close to your body, the hand reaching to point (7). Try to keep facing forward. Your left arm and leg are closely behind in counter-tension. The movement from (6) to (7) has a flat stress as it originates from the Table Plane.

85

● *Pathway 8:* Your right leg
now moves to the centre and
forward as your right arm
reaches to point Forward/High (8)
The counter-tension is very clear
with your left arm and leg in Back/
Deep. The movement from (7) to (8)
has a steep stress as it originates from
the Door Plane.

● *Pathway 9:*
From point
High/Forward your right arm moves
to point Right/Back (9) at medium
level. Your right foot steps to the
Right/Back, taking weight. As with
all medium levels, strive for a
horizontal line. In this case, your left
arm and leg are in Left/Forward
providing a strong counter-tension.
The movement from (8) to (9) has
a flowing stress as it originates from
the Wheel Plane.

86

● *Pathway 10:* Your movement now takes you to Left/High. Your right arm crosses at approximately chin level to point Left/High (10) as your right leg crosses closely in front of your left leg and the right foot takes weight with the heel slightly raised off the ground. Try to remain facing forward. Your left arm and leg are in counter-tension. The movement from (9) to (10) has a flat stress as it originates in the Table Plane.

● *Pathway 11:* Your right leg now moves directly to the point Deep/Forward (11) taking weight on its bent knee whilst your right arm also stretches into this direction. Your left arm is in counter-tension behind and your left leg is probably raised off the ground, depending how far forward you are reaching. The movement from (10) to (11) has a steep stress as it originates from the Door Plane.

● *Pathway 12:* From Deep/Forward your right leg crosses behind your left leg and takes the weight as your right arm goes under your left armpit and stretches into point Left/Back (12), your body arching slightly over Left/Back. Your left arm and leg provide a strong counter-tension as your body is 'pulled' into a horizontal position. The movement from (11) to (12) has a flowing stress as it originates from the Wheel Plane. This last position (12) was the position you took up when starting the Right 'A' Scale, in preparation for the first movement pathway.

## The Flowing Version of the Right Side

Now you can enjoy following the curving pathways of this scale which are beautiful in their harmonious relatedness. Taking a few steps along each of the curved pathways enhances the three different stresses of 'flat', 'steep' and 'flowing' (see Figure 41, opposite).

## The 'A' Scale for the Left Side

● *Preparation:* From stance, step back with your left foot crossing behind the right leg to the Right/Deep/Back corner. Simultaneously, take your left hand under the right arm to reach towards point Right/Back (12) of the Table Plane. Your right arm and leg are in counter-tension.

● *Pathway 1:* From Right/Back, your left arm moves to point Left/High (1) of the Door Plane. Your left leg steps to the left, your left foot taking weight with your heel slightly raised off the floor but not fully balanced on the ball of the foot as in demi-pointe. Meanwhile your right side is in counter-tension.

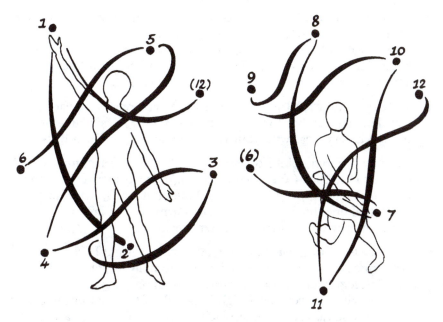

Figure 41: Flowing Version of the 'A' Scale

- *Pathway 2*: From Left/High, the pathway moves your left arm and leg to point Deep/Back (2) of the Wheel plane. The Deep/Back position lifts your right leg in its forward counter-tension position.

- *Pathway 3*: From Deep/Back your left arm and leg cross over to the right side in front, your arm moving into point Right/Forward (3) of the Table Plane. Try to keep facing front. Your body is almost horizontal at this medium level. Your right leg (knee slightly bent) is sufficiently inclined to the left side in counter-tension for you to look over your left shoulder at the right foot.

- *Pathway 4:* Your next movement takes you to point Left/Deep (4) of the Door Plane. Your left leg is in a deep bend, your left arm reaches to point (4). Your right leg is partially outstretched and the arm raised in counter-tension.

- *Pathway 5:* Your left leg steps centre back as your left arm moves to point High/Back (5). The counter-tension is Deep/Forward.

- *Pathway 6:* Your left arm is going to move to Left/Forward (6) as the left leg steps in the same direction. At medium level, your body can attempt to take up a horizontal position, lifting your right leg and arm backwards in counter-tension.

89

- *Pathway 7:* Your left arm and leg are going to move across, in front of your body, to point Right/Deep (7). Your left knee is bent and takes weight whilst your left arm crosses close to your body, the hand reaching to point (7). Try to keep facing forward. Your right arm and leg are closely behind in counter-tension.

- *Pathway 8:* Your left leg now moves to the centre and forward as your left arm reaches to point Forward/High (8) The counter-tension is very clear with your right arm and leg in Deep/Back.

- *Pathway 9:* From point Forward/High (8) your left arm moves to point Left/Back (9) at medium level. Your left foot steps to the Left/Back, taking weight. As with all medium levels, strive for a horizontal line. In this case, your right arm and leg are in Right/Forward providing a strong counter-tension.

- *Pathway 10:* Your movement now takes you to Right/High. Your left arm crosses at approximately chin level to point Right/High (10) as your left leg crosses closely in front of your right leg and your foot takes weight with your heel slightly raised off the floor but not fully on demi-pointe. Try to remain facing forward. Your right arm and leg are in counter-tension.

- *Pathway 11:* Your left leg now moves directly to the point Forward/Deep (11) taking weight on its bent knee whilst your left arm also stretches into this direction. Your right arm is in counter-tension behind and your right leg is probably raised off the ground, depending how far forward you are reaching.

- *Pathway 12:* From Forward/Deep your left leg crosses behind your right leg and takes weight as your left arm goes under your right armpit and stretches into point Right/Back (12), your body arching over Right/Back. Your right arm and leg provide a strong counter-tension as this is medium level and your body is 'pulled' into a horizontal position. Once again, you reach the first position (12) from which you started.


### The Flowing Version for the Left Side

- As in the Flowing Version of the right side leading, follow the pathways, substituting Left for Right, in a smooth, harmonious way.

## THE 'B' SCALE

The 'B' Scale is much more dynamic than the 'A' Scale, requiring strength and force, and is therefore considered to be the man's scale, but there is no reason why everyone should not try it. It contains the same inclinations of flat, steep and flowing as the 'A' Scale, though in a different order. As you work through it, you will discover that the four flat inclinations you met in the 'A' Scale have now changed to four different flat inclinations.

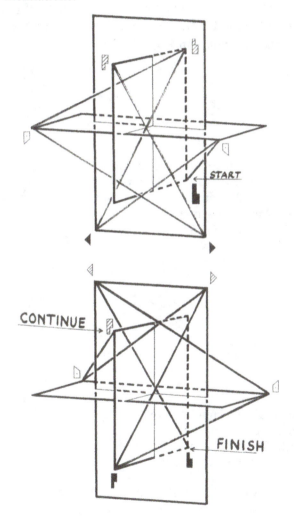

Figure 42: The first six pathways and the second six pathways of the 'B' Scale

As with the 'A' Scale, the leading foot will momentarily transfer weight to the other foot before it moves into each new direction. The non-leading side will, as before, move into counter-tension. In the deep zone, the knees bend. Remember the directional sign relates to the pathway immediately preceding the signal point.

### The 'B' Scale for the Right Side

As in the 'A' Scale, our starting position will be the last point of the scale i.e. Deep/Forward. This allows us to move along the whole length of the first pathway ending in Right/Back.

● *Preparation.* From stance, step forward with your right foot to Deep/Forward and reach towards the same point with your right arm. Your left arm and leg should be raised in counter-tension.

● *Pathway 1.* Take a step back to open Right/Deep and stretch into Right/Back with your right arm (Table Plane). Your left arm and leg are raised in counter-tension as your body assumes an almost horizontal level.

● *Pathway 2:* From Right/Deep/Back your right foot (knee bent) moves into a Left/Deep crossing position whilst your right arm reaches across your chest to the same point, Left/Deep of the Door Plane. Try to keep facing the front. Your left arm and leg are crossed behind in counter-tension. The movement from Right/Back to Left/Deep has a flat stress as it originates from the Table Plane.

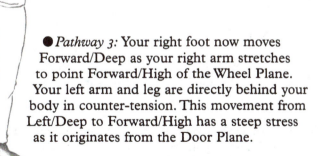

●*Pathway 3:* Your right foot now moves Forward/Deep as your right arm stretches to point Forward/High of the Wheel Plane. Your left arm and leg are directly behind your body in counter-tension. This movement from Left/Deep to Forward/High has a steep stress as it originates from the Door Plane.

- *Pathway 4:* Your right leg now crosses behind your left leg as it steps back into Left/Deep taking the weight (knee slightly bent) as your right arm moves across your body, your right hand moving under your left armpit, reaching towards point Left/Back of the Table Plane. Your left arm and leg are crossed in front in counter-tension. The movement from Forward/High to Left/Back has a flowing stress as it originates from the Wheel Plane.

- *Pathway 5:* Your right leg now moves to open position Right/Deep (knee bent) as your right arm reaches towards point Right/Deep of the Door Plane. Your left arm and leg are in open counter-tension. This movement from Left/Back to Right/Deep has a flat stress as it originates from the Table Plane.

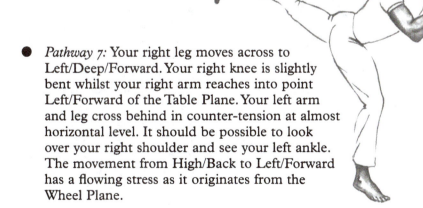

● *Pathway 6:* Your right leg moves Deep/Back whilst your right arm stretches towards point High/Back of the Wheel plane. Your left arm and leg are forward in counter-tension. The movement from Right/Deep to High/Back has a steep stress as it originates from the Door Plane.

● *Pathway 7:* Your right leg moves across to Left/Deep/Forward. Your right knee is slightly bent whilst your right arm reaches into point Left/Forward of the Table Plane. Your left arm and leg cross behind in counter-tension at almost horizontal level. It should be possible to look over your right shoulder and see your left ankle. The movement from High/Back to Left/Forward has a flowing stress as it originates from the Wheel Plane.

● *Pathway 8:* Your right foot moves to an open right sideways position, your heel raised just off the floor whilst your right arm is stretching towards point Right/High of the Door Plane. Your left arm and leg are in counter-tension. The movement from Left/Forward to Right/High has a flat stress as it originates from the Table Plane.

● *Pathway 9:* Your right leg now moves to Back/Deep (knee bent) whilst your right arm reaches towards the same point of the Wheel Plane. Try to keep facing forward. Your left arm and leg are raised in forward counter-tension. The movement from Right/High to Back/Deep has a steep stress as it originates from the Door Plane.

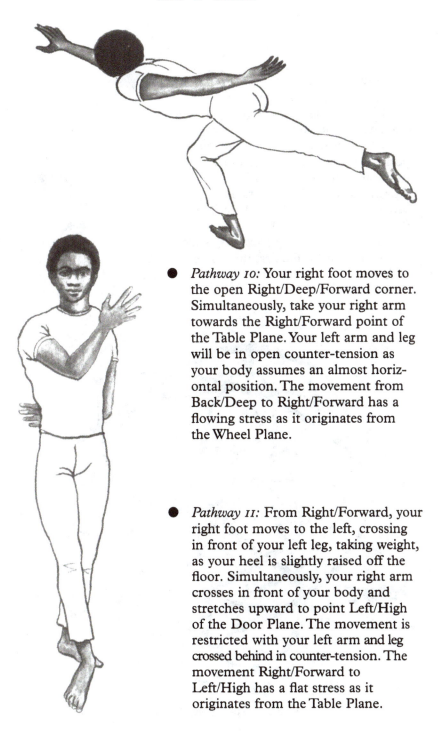

● *Pathway 10:* Your right foot moves to
the open Right/Deep/Forward corner.
Simultaneously, take your right arm
towards the Right/Forward point of
the Table Plane. Your left arm and leg
will be in open counter-tension as
your body assumes an almost horizontal position. The movement from
Back/Deep to Right/Forward has a
flowing stress as it originates from
the Wheel Plane.

● *Pathway 11:* From Right/Forward, your
right foot moves to the left, crossing
in front of your left leg, taking weight,
as your heel is slightly raised off the
floor. Simultaneously, your right arm
crosses in front of your body and
stretches upward to point Left/High
of the Door Plane. The movement is
restricted with your left arm and leg
crossed behind in counter-tension. The
movement Right/Forward to
Left/High has a flat stress as it
originates from the Table Plane.

97

● *Pathway 12:* From Left/
High, your right foot moves to
Deep/Forward and your right arm
stretches to the point Deep/Forward of
the Wheel Plane. This Deep/Forward
position raises your left leg and arm in a
backward counter-tension. The
movement has a steep stress as it
originates from the Door Plane. This is
the position from which you started
at the beginning of the Right 'B' Scale,
in preparation for the first movement
pathway.

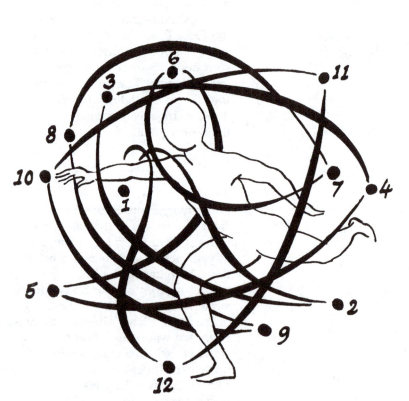

Figure 43: The flowing 'B' Scale

## The Flowing Version for the Right Side

● Work through the scale, flowing harmoniously from one point to the next (see Figure 43, opposite).

## The 'B' Scale for the Left Side

● *Preparation:* From stance, step forward with your left foot to Deep/Forward and reach towards the same point with your left arm. Your right arm and leg should be raised in counter-tension.

● *Pathway 1:* Take a step back to open Left/Deep, and stretch into Left/Back with your left arm (Table Plane). The right arm and leg are raised in counter-tension as the body assumes an almost horizontal level.

● *Pathhway 2:* From Left/Back/Deep corner your left foot (knee bent) moves into a Right/Deep crossing position whilst your left arm reaches across the chest to the same point, Right/Deep of the Door Plane. Try to keep facing the front. Your right arm and leg are crossed behind in counter-tension.

● *Pathway 3:* Your left foot now moves Forward/Deep as your left arm stretches to point Forward/High of the Wheel Plane. Your right arm and leg are directly behind your body in counter-tension.

● *Pathway 4:* Your left leg now crosses behind your right leg as it steps back into Right/Deep taking the weight (knee slightly bent) as your left arm moves across your body, your left hand moving under your right armpit, reaching towards point Right/Back of the Table Plane. Your right arm and leg are crossed in front in counter-tension.

● *Pathway 5:* Your left leg now moves into open position Left/Deep (knee bent) as your left arm reaches towards point Left/Deep of the Door Plane. Your right arm and leg are in counter-tension.

● *Pathway 6:* Your left leg moves Deep/Back whilst your left arm stretches towards point High/Back of the Wheel Plane. Your right arm and leg are forward in counter-tension.

● *Pathway 7:* Your left leg moves across to Right/Deep/Forward. Your left knee is slightly bent whilst your left arm reaches to point Right/Forward of the Table Plane. Your right arm and leg cross behind in counter-tension at almost horizontal level. It should be possible to look over your left shoulder at your right ankle.

● *Pathway 8:* Your left foot moves to open left sideways position, your heel raised just off the floor whilst your left arm is stretching towards point Left/High of the Door Plane. Your right arm and leg are in counter-tension.

● *Pathway 9:* Your left leg now moves to Back/Deep (knee bent) whilst your left arm reaches towards the same point of the Wheel Plane. Try to keep facing forward. Your right arm and leg are raised in forward counter-tension.

● *Pathway 10:* Your left foot moves to the open Left/Deep/Forward corner. Simultaneously, take your left arm towards the Left/Forward point of the Table Plane. Your right arm and leg will be in open counter-tension as the body assumes an almost horizontal position.

● *Pathway 11:* From Left/Forward, your left foot moves to the right, crossing in front of your right leg, taking weight, as your heel is slightly raised off the floor. Simultaneously, your left arm crosses in front of your body and stretches upward to point Right/High of the Door Plane. The movement is restricted with your right arm and leg crossed behind in counter-tension.

● *Pathway 12:* From Right/High, your left foot moves to Deep/Forward and the left arm stretches to point Deep/Forward of the Wheel Plane, while your right leg and arm are raised in a backward counter-tension. Once again, you reach the first position from which you started.

### The Flowing Version for the Left Side

● As in the Flowing Version of the right side leading, work through the scale, flowing harmoniously from one point to the next.

## STEEPLES AND VOLUTES

Before leaving the 'A' and 'B' Scales, it is interesting to observe that, not only do the pathways link the three Planes in rotation, each having its own expressive quality of flat, steep or flowing, but the pathways also incline towards one or more diagonals in angles that are either acute (steeples), or obtuse (volutes). You may remember that the Dimensional Cross is the 'norm' and, therefore, every other movement pathway is a deflection from the norm. Starting with the Right 'A' Scale as a guide (see diagram on page 81) let us discover a little more about the inner mysteries of the Scales.

### Steeples

*The 'A' Scale. Right side leading.*

● With the right side leading and following the pathways in their normal sequence, starting in Left/Back (12), we move to Right/High (1) and then to Back/Deep (2). These two movement pathways describe an acute (narrow, sharp) angle which has its apex inclining towards the Right/High/Forward Diagonal. In movement, the influence of the diagonal is clearly felt.

● Continuing from Back/Deep (2) the next two pathways travel to Left/Forward (3) and on to Right/Deep (4). This time, the apex inclines the Diagonal Left/High/Forward. In movement, the influence of the second Diagonal Scale can be clearly felt. This is the second steeple.

● Keeping to this pattern of exploration, try working through the whole 'A' Scale, discovering the steeples for yourself. You will find that there is one diagonal missing from the the 'A' Scale. (Remember that the 8 diagonals of the Diagonal Scale can start from the top or the bottom zones.) The missing diagonal, in this case, Right/High/Back to Left/Deep/Forward, is considered as the 'axis' around which the pathways are situated. After completing the right side for the remaining steeples, try working through the Left 'A' Scale for steeples and find the 'missing diagonal' for yourself.

*The 'B' Scale. Right side leading.*

● Starting in Forward/Deep, the first pathway leads Right/Back and then to Left/Deep. The apex of the angle is inclined towards the Diagonal Right/High/Back. This is your first steeple for the Right 'B' Scale.

● From Left/Deep the first pathway moves to Forward/High and secondly, to Left/Backward. The apex of the angle is inclined towards the Right/High/Forward Diagonal. This is your second steeple for the Right 'B' Scale. The sharp angularity of the angles can be distinctly seen and are clearly felt in the body when moving along these pathways.

● Continue along this way to discover the remaining steeples, remembering the order of the pathways. (Your next steeple will start at Left/Back and move to Right/Deep and then to Back/High.) Where is the apex? From moving along these pathways, you will discover the inclination and the diagonal. The missing diagonal providing the axis for the Right 'B' Scale is from Left/High/Forward to Right/Deep/Back.

● Now try working through the steeples of the Left 'B' Scale and discover the 'missing' diagonal for that side.

**Volutes**

*'A' Scale. Right side leading.*

● Starting from Right/High (1) of the 'A' Scale, the movement takes you down to Deep/Back (2). This single pathway inclines towards the Right/High/Forward Diagonal. The second pathway (completing the angle) goes on to Left/Forward (3). The deflection has changed and the inclination is now towards a second Diagonal, Right/Deep/Backward. (The Left/High/Forward Diagonal in reverse.) Clearly, this is not an acute angle but an obtuse angle. In movement it is felt to have a much wider curve. This wider curving angle occurs when two different diagonals influence two consecutive movement pathways. The resulting obtuse angle is known as a volute.

● From Left/Forward (3) the movement goes to Right/Deep (4). This single pathway inclines towards the Left/High/Forward Diagonal. The second pathway completing the angle goes to High/Back (5) and inclines towards a new diagonal from Right/Deep/Forward to Left/High/Backward. The inclination is clearly felt when moving along this pathway. This is your second volute for the 'A' Scale.

● Following this pattern, try to work through the rest of the scale, taking each volute in two separate movements. You will find that one diagonal is missing and this is the 'axis' for the scale. It is again the Right/High/Back to Left/Deep/Forward.

● Work through the 'A' Scale for the left side and discover for yourself which is the missing diagonal.

*The 'B' Scale. Right side leading.*

● Starting from the crossed position, Left/High, move to Deep/Forward. The single movement inclines towards the Left/High/Back Diagonal. Continuing along the next pathway to complete the angle, your movement takes you to Right/Back. This movement inclines from Left/Deep/Forward to Right/Back and is the first volute. It is an obtuse angle because it has inclinations towards, not one, but two diagonals.

● From your last position Right/Back, the next pathway leads to Left/Deep. The movement inclines towards the Diagonal Left/Deep/Forward. The second pathway completing this angle moves on to High/Forward and inclines towards the Right/High/Forward Diagonal. This is the second volute of the 'B' Scale; it also has inclinations towards two diagonals.

● Continue in the same pattern through the rest of the scale. You will find that the missing diagonal, providing the axis for the scale, is Left/High/Forward to Right/Deep/Back.

● Now work through the volutes for the Left 'B' Scale and discover the 'missing' diagonal providing the axis for the left side of the 'B' Scale.

Volutes and steeples can, of course, be used freely as dance motifs.

## THE MISSING DIAGONALS

Laban stated that, 'Whilst three of the four diagonals of each of the 'A' and 'B' Scales have an active role, it is the fourth diagonal that determines the expressive character of the scale and can be considered its 'backbone'. It acts as the axis for the pathways, distinguishing one scale from another. The axis for the 'A' Scale (right side) is the fourth

Diagonal Right/High/Back ◣ to Left/Deep/Forward ◣ . For example (and here we will use some notation):

- The first volute (steep/flowing) travels from Right/High ◿ via Back/Deep ◤ to Left/Forward ◹ . Instead of taking this as a circuitous pathway, we will take a direct path from Right/High ◿ to Left/Forward ◹ . This direct flat connection is a flat deflection of the missing Diagonal Right/High/Back ◣ to Left/Deep/ Forward ◣ in reverse, as it is going **towards** the Right-Left Plane and not coming **away from** it.

- The second volute (flat/steep) moves from Left/Forward ◹ via Right/Deep ◢ to Back/High ◺ . Taking a direct path, as with the first volute, we move from Left/Forward ◹ to Back/High ◺ , so we have a flowing deflection from the missing diagonal Right/High/Back ◣ to Left/Deep/Forward ◣ . It is an inclination in reverse of the Diagonal Scale.

- The third volute (flowing/flat) moves from Back/High ◺ via Right/Forward ◹ to Left/Deep ◀ . The direct path moves from Back/High ◺ to Left/Deep ◀ giving us a steep deflection from the missing diagonal Right/High/Back ◣ to Left/Deep/ Forward ◣ also in reverse.

These three volutes, each comprising of two transversals, making six transversals in all, represent half the Right 'A' Scale. As the second half of the scale is parallel to the first half, the direct connections of each volute will also be parallel. Each volute has a circuitous pathway around the missing diagonal which forms the axis of the Right 'A' Scale. It should now be possible to work through the Left 'A' Scale for yourselves.

In the Right 'A' Scale the missing diagonal Right/High/Back to Left/Deep/Forward is the one in which the right side of the body would have naturally exerted the greatest strength. The other three diagonals, which do appear, seem to block strong movements when the right side is leading. Consequently, the expressive character of this scale is moderate and rather soft. This also applies to the Left 'A' Scale; its character is also moderate and rather soft.

In the Right 'B' Scale, the missing diagonal Left/High/Forward to Right/Deep/Back encourages a more gentle quality of movement, and the three diagonals that do appear seem to block more gentle movements. Consequently, the expressive character of the 'B' Scale is stronger and more dynamic than that of the 'A' Scale. In both cases, the expressive character is conditioned by its emplacement in space. This also applies to the Left 'B' Scale, its expressive quality is strong and dynamic.

## THE COMPOSITION OF THE PRIMARY SCALE

It helps to remember that:-

i.  Diagonals go through the centre of the body and kinesphere moving, simultaneously, into three directions.

ii.  Transversals do not go through the centre of the body or the kinesphere.

iii.  Surface-lines make up the frame-work of the icosahedron and link the 12 signal points of the three planes.

iv.  Diameters go through the centre of the body and kinesphere moving, simultaneously, into two directions.

Each end of a diagonal 'pierces' the centre of a triangular face of the icosahedron. Let us take the diagonal L/D/F ▟ to R/H/B ◪ as an example:

1.  R/H/B ◪ goes through the centre of a triangular face comprising of 3 signal points, one from each of the three planes, R/H (Door Plane), R/B (Table Plane), H/B (Wheel Plane).

2.  L/D/F ▟ also goes through the centre of a triangular face comprising of three signal points, one from each of the three planes: L/D (Door plane), L/F (Table plane), F/D (Wheel plane).

The contrasting triangular faces at each end of a diagonal are called **polar triangles** (see Figure 44, opposite).

Laban called a chain of 6 transversals surrounding a diagonal axis, a **cluster** (see Figure 45, opposite). He likened the diagonal's axis to the axis of the earth. The earth rotates around a tilted axis. Similarly, the diagonal has a tilted axis and is encircled at each end by a polar triangle. Between them lies the cluster chain which makes similar revolving movements.

Laban suggested that, 'movements which follow the chain of the cluster are seen in nature, in animals in captivity, or in the swaying of a drunken man, or one who is tired and falling asleep. **It is, in general, an unconscious and involuntary movement.'**

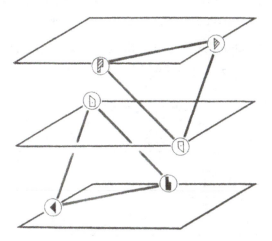

Figure 44: The Two Polar Triangles

(i) ◀ · · · ◗ · · · ▮ · · · | ◀

(ii) ▷ · · · ◖ · · · ◢ · · · | ▷

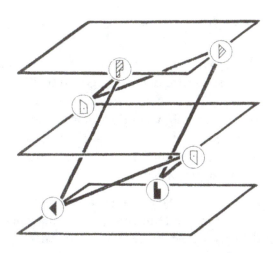

Figure 45: The Cluster

◀ · · · ◢ · · · ◗ · · · ▷ · · · ▮ · · · ◖ · · · | ◀

Besides each diagonal being surrounded by a chain of 6 transversals (a cluster), it is also surrounded by a chain of 6 surface-lines.

Laban called the chain of 6 surface-lines a **girdle**.(The surface-lines can also be arranged in 3 parallel pairs.)

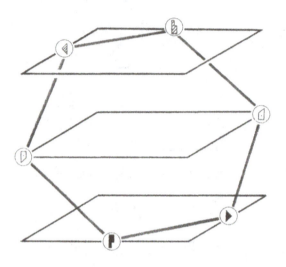

Figure 46:The Girdle

The **girdle**, circling around the icosahedron, touching the 6 surface-lines, corresponds to the equator. Laban suggested that, ' . . . movements which follow the girdle are seen in nature in emphatic gestures and actions. They are, in general, voluntary movements. The emphasis contains, however, a certain state of unconscious excitement, but this excitement is a kind of day-dream. Man is awake in the equatorial, and not asleep in the axial cluster movements.'

These two strongly contrasting attitudes remind us of the strongly contrasting movements in the Dimensional and Diagonal Scales. The Dimensional and Diagonal Scales represent extremes in stability and lability which are rarely employed in everyday actions. Involuntary movements can be clearly seen in the distressed behaviour of many caged animals, the efforts of a drunken man trying to regain his equilibrium and the exhausted man determined to fight a natural tendency to relax into sleep. Voluntary movements, arising from an excited state of mind, change ordinary gestures and actions into more emphatic behaviour.

There is a third mode of movement which links these two sharply contrasting modes of the cluster chain and the girdle chain. This third mode moves alternately from one cluster point to a girdle point and so on, alternately. (And vice versa.) This third mode occurs naturally in our daily activities. Occasionally, however, sudden, uncontrolled outbursts make the movement jump and our emotions take over for a time. When this happens, our movement becomes caught up, either in the involuntary behaviour of the cluster chain only or, at other times, our movement becomes caught up in the girdle chain, displaying emphatic behaviour. This latter behaviour can be seen in such activities as dancing and fighting. Sudden outbursts generally return to the more everyday behaviour associated with the third mode which we call the **Primary** (or **Standard**) **Scale**. The pathways move around the periphery of the icosahederon. The natural chain sequence of the Primary Scale counterbalances the automation associated with the cluster and the emphatic associated with the girdle.

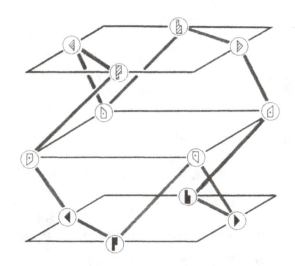

Figure 47: The Primary Scale

The above shows a chain of 12 peripheral surface-lines revolving around the axis of the diagonal L/D/F to R/H/B notation.

## The Primary Scale for the Right Side

As with the other scales, the right foot will step into each new direction after momentarily shifting weight to the left foot. The left side of the body will be in counter-tension.

- *Preparation.* From stance, take up the last point of the scale so that you can move through the whole length of the first pathway. Step forward and reach Forward/High with your right arm.

- *Pathway 1.* Step to the right with your right foot and reach Right/High with your right arm.

- *Pathway 2.* Step Right/Forward with your right foot and reach out to Right/Forward (Table Plane) with your right arm, your body inclining towards horizontal level.

- *Pathway 3.* Your next movement takes your right foot to Deep/Forward and your right arm also to Deep/Forward (Wheel Plane).

- *Pathway 4.* Step back with your right leg to Right/Deep , your right arm stretching into Right Deep ( Door Plane).

- *Pathway 5.* Your right leg steps to Right/Back. Your right arm moves to Right/Back (Table Plane).

- *Pathway 6.* Your right leg moves to Deep/Back and your right arm moves into Deep/Back (Wheel Plane).

- *Pathway 7.* Your right leg and arm cross over in front of the left leg and stretch to Left/Deep (Door Plane).

- *Pathway 8.* Your right foot goes to Left/Back as your right arm also moves to Left/Back (Table Plane).

- *Pathway 9.* Your right leg moves back and your right arm moves to High/Back (Wheel Plane).

- *Pathway 10.* Your right leg steps across to Left/High as your right arm also moves to Left/High ( Door Plane).

- *Pathway 11.* Your right leg moves to Left/Forward and your right arm moves into Left/Forward (Table Plane).

- *Pathway 12.* Your right leg steps forward and your right arm moves to High/Forward (Wheel Plane). This is where you started the Primary Scale.

*Note:* Before we leave the immensity of the icosahedron, it may interest you to know that at the end of this book there are instructions on How to Make Your Own Icosahedron.

# 3

# *Space, Time Weight and Flow*

## SPACE

Space is a difficult word to define. Ask twenty people their opinion as to what space means to them and you will most likely get twenty different answers. We are constantly learning about *outer* space, and we know that telescopes and instruments have probed far into it, but it is something so vast and boundless that it is still incomprehensible to most of us.

On a more down to earth level, in order to comprehend the space we inhabit we need certain visual signposts such as walls or fences or boundaries or recognisable objects so that we can tell whether we are in a large space or small space. To pinpoint exactly where we are in space we need three co-ordinates: the distance we are from, say, the wall in front of us, combined with the distance we are from, say, the wall to our right, combined with the height we are from the ground. We also know that the space we live and breathe in is not just an empty void but is crammed with air molecules – not so tangible as water molecules but plainly evident if we wave a flat hand violently in the air. We need space to be able to move and when we do our bodies displace space. When we take a step we push some space out of the way and, as we do so, space fills where we have just stood. As well as this, motion in space exists within us. Whilst the human body lives, it breathes; the heart and pulse have their rhythms and the blood circulates. These movements are a proof of life.

Let us consider the space around us for a moment – our personal space, our kinesphere. We can minimise our use of it by bending all our joints and curling up into a ball. In contrast, we can fling ourselves all over the place, extending the whole body and stretching our legs, arms and fingers as far as they will go. This contracting and expanding of the body and its parts, Laban called **gathering** and **scattering**. Not only the body but also its individual parts have the capacity to gather and scatter, particularly arms. When we open our arms wide to welcome an old friend, the movement is of scattering – scattering any doubts that we are pleased to see them. When we clasp them and give them a hug, that is gathering. Fingers and thumbs can clench into a gathering movement or throw themselves open in a scattering movement. Legs can kick out in a scattering movement or pull inwards in a gathering movement.

Everybody has an individual way of moving and using space according to their genes, their build, their temperament and their personal approach. They will move but they may not necessarily move well. Unfortunately, there is no system of learning movement as we grow up; we just imitate those we see around us. If the role-model is good, the result is likely to be better than if the role-model is bad. This is more obvious where learning to speak is concerned but more of that later.

Although Laban dismissed the idea that he 'invented' the Art of Movement, his great achievement was that he made us realise the value of studying and practising movement as an art. Hitherto, movement study, right from the days of the ancient Greeks, was mostly confined to gymnastics of one kind or another, or to dancing, either of which might enhance our everyday movements or might not. Now, with the inspiration of Laban and our consciousness of the dimensional cross, we can explore our potential in a bid to extend our range of movement at all times, not just when performing gymnastics or dancing.

Unlike most animals, we are able to choose how we want to move. We can move straight to where we want to go or meander there in a flexible manner. In order to move at all, our bodies need Space. The most flexible movements we make require us to bend and twist our joints; such movements need to occur close to the body. As our limbs extend further away from our bodies into space, they become less flexible and more and more direct. Of course, being crammed into a lift with a lot of people, it doesn't matter how flexible you are, you will not be able to move. On the other hand, there are some individuals who are so rigid in their movement that they might just as well be jammed into a lift for all the space they use.

Finally, as we move about in our space, whether it be walking the long path home or merely reaching for the telephone, the use of focus is of paramount importance. Without focus we can very easily lose our way and never reach our goal.

### Some Examples

● 1a. Moving directly in space as when running a race.

● b. Moving indirectly in a flexible manner as when walking down a crowded street.

● c. Fear of using the surrounding space. This is evident with people who continually cross their arms in front of their bodies, often clenching their hands tightly round their forearms. Similarly, when sitting, they will tightly cross their legs and, if they are particularly thin and nervous, they can be seen to twist their ankles round each other as well.

### Exercises for Exploring your Space

● 1a. Imagine you are meeting a special friend off a train. As soon as you recognise him or her in the crowd, your attention is focused and, ignoring everyone else, you make directly for your friend. If there is sufficient room, taking into account that the platform is crowded, you open your arms wide before giving an affectionate hug.

● b. Imagine you are in a crowded market or souk. You have no particular intention of buying anything and you wander aimlessly from stall to stall, sometimes crossing over to those opposite. Every now and then an article vaguely interests you and you examine it rather casually to avoid attracting the stallholder's attention. As he hovers near, you put the item down and saunter off.

● c. You are a painfully shy person entering a room full of strangers. Everything about you is inhibited and awkward. All the other people seem to know each other from the way they are talking and laughing. However, they totally ignore you, sometimes knocking into you without a word of apology, making you feel even more alienated and wretched. One could resolve this sad story by adding that you are in actual fact a celebrated but reclusive figure and when this is discovered everyone falls over themselves to ingratiate themselves to you but perhaps this should wait till later on in the book!

## TIME

Time and space were once considered two separate entities; time was pronounced absolute while space was not absolute. Even so, space and time are inextricably linked. Time, though, was easier to measure than distance. In earlier civilisations, time was measured by astronomy and the seasons whereas space could only be measured by paces. The sun and moon dictated whether it was night or day while mankind, like the plants around him, travelled from babyhood, to youth, maturity and old age, as he still does.

The passing of a year could also be measured by observing the seasons. The New Year saw the frosts disappearing as the earth warmed up from its long sleep. Spring's arrival meant it was time to sow crops and tend the delicate seedlings. Summer brought an end to the countryman's long labours caring for his growing crops. As it slipped gently into autumn it became a time for celebration and thanksgiving for the harvest safely gathered. Man and beast were assured of food during the long, dark winter as the earth rested. The cycle was complete. In ancient times the ritual dances reflected man's relationship with the four seasons. In those days, dance was not a profession or a hobby but a living tradition passed on from generation to generation, the remnants of which can still be seen in Bali and a few other countries.

Both space and time need measuring devices to get a 'purchase' on the 'where' and 'when' and, since the discovery that light travels at a fixed speed (186,000 miles per second), enormous distances can be precisely calculated with the help of cesium clocks. (Have we not been informed recently that the Andromeda Galaxy which we can actually see with the naked eye is four-and-a-half billion light years away?) Einstein persuaded us to abandon the idea of absolute time, emphasising the fact that light is the only finite entity in existence and from the theory of relativity was born the concept of space-time – space-time being the combination of the three co-ordinates of space plus the co-ordinate of time. Now, however, the theory of relativity is in danger of being eclipsed by the notion that both space and time are no more than illusions. The very foundations of physics are being rocked by the emergence of the string theory where the universe consists of tiny vibrating strings. If this is so, then vibrating strings bring us neatly back to Pythagoras. All this, of course, doesn't help us to time the speed of a pirouette or a golf swing, but how heartened Laban would have been to find that his belief in the relevance of the cosmos to our lives is constantly emerging.

Today, it seems time dictates how we should plan our day. We have alarm clocks to wake us, public clocks and wrist watches to see we 'aren't late'. Modern clocks, as well as dividing time into hours, minutes and seconds, can now show us micro-seconds flying past, seeming to emphasise the brevity of our lives. Yet clocks have become essential to most of us, especially those who work in business or commerce. Eyes are constantly on clocks for keeping business appointments or catching flights. Without clocks we would find it difficult to measure the duration of time accurately.

Yet, though we are surrounded by watches and clocks, everyone responds to time in different ways because our own inbuilt clocks vary enormously. Some people are naturally slow and sustained in their movements while others are naturally quick and sudden. Those individuals who can choose their occupation will most likely gravitate towards tasks that suit their movement speed but slow movers would be ill-advised to try their hand on the floor of the Stock Exchange, where lightning decisions and darting movements are the order of the day, just as the quick, impulsive mover would most likely not make a success at being a potter where a certain amount of calm patience is required.

In music, time is measured in the note values of minims, crotchets, quavers, semi-quavers and even lesser denominations. Although these units of time vary in duration one from the other, their values in relation to each other remain constant. These notes indicate not only pitch but rhythmic patterns which can be anything from a march to a waltz. Most people move to music at some time or other. Usually music follows a regular rhythmic pattern which is easy to move to. Sometimes the music speeds up or slows down but the rhythm is still metrical. Sometimes the music is in an odd rhythm but the same amount of beats in a bar (seven beats in a bar may seem tricky to a morris dancer but it won't worry a Greek). At other times, the music may constantly change rhythm, making it very free to move to but actually more difficult. Most of our everyday movements are carried out in a free a-rhythmic way and, indeed, we can dance without music in a free a-rhythmic way. A movement not bound by metricality is said to have a free, irregular time-rhythm, often leading where dance is concerned, to more expressive, dynamic interpretation. Of course, there are occasions when one can move very expressively to music as in dance, where the legs and feet will prefer to follow the music's metricality whilst the upper body and arms will follow a more irregular time-rhythm. Ideally, a performer should be able to express both the qualities of regular (metric) and irregular (free) time-rhythm. Many people do not perform, of course, but nevertheless, there is rhythm in their actions.

What, you may say, is rhythm? Laban tells us that 'rhythm is the lawless law which governs us all without exception. But only a few are familiar with it, although it is always around us and within us and reveals itself everywhere'. Time and rhythm are inseparable. Rhythm consists of accented and unaccented moments in time. We tend to think of rhythm as something audible, but it can also be purely visual; a daffodil nodding in the breeze has its own rhythm. As for a regular rhythm the one that is fundamental to us all is the heart-beat. Each of us will have our own pace but, in repose, the heart beats regularly. This, however, will accelerate with strong muscular activity or an emotional change such as excitement or severe nerves like stagefright. The other great example of rhythm that is within us is breathing. Like the heart-beat, in repose or sleep, the breathing rhythm is regular and almost imperceptible, according to the demand for oxygen. But with increased activity the speed of the breathing will also increase and be more perceptible. So, the two great rhythms that are central to our lives are the heart-beat and that of the breath.

Some people are described as having no sense of rhythm, probably because they appear not to be able to move to a regular beat and are therefore given up as hopeless. But are they? They have a heart-beat and they have a breath pulse. If not pressurised, they will undoubtedly be able to tap out a regular beat on a table. The most fundamental rhythm that we all perform is walking, which takes on a regular beat, once we get into our stride. As for marching, it is far easier to march on the beat than off, even if one finds oneself on the wrong foot! Having no sense of rhythm is similar to having no sense of pitch and that is because the sense has not been given enough time to respond to the demand. There should be time to be at ease with ourselves so that our sense of geography (where) and geometry (proportion) and time itself (when) are all in accord and become one.

We all know the duration of a movement, or series of movements, can range from very short to very long, just as the speed of a movement, or series of movements, can range from very fast to very slow. Examples of very short movements are blinking (usually involuntary), flicking a piece of fluff off your coat or jumping out of the way of a fast car coming suddenly round the corner. Movements that are of necessity slow are more difficult to pinpoint. Yawning is definitely slow (and also involuntary). Feeling the texture of something precious, of necessity, is slow. Waving to someone nearby would probably be fairly quick and lively, but the further away they were would cause the wave to be slower and more expansive (imagine waving to someone across a valley or a lake). Some movements start slowly and increase in speed such as a golf swing. The slow beginning consists of raising the golf club and taking aim; once the decision is made the stroke is lightning fast. Note also that the breath is taken in slowly with the preparation and exhaled quickly with the shot. Most movements where a precise aim needs to be taken first will commence slowly. An example of a fast movement slowing down also comes from the world of sport: when a runner, employing a series of fast movements wins the race, once past the winning post, he doesn't suddenly stop running but gradually slows down.

## WEIGHT

Weight, we are told, is the force exerted on a body by a gravitational field; our ability to stand upright depends on the tension between the force of the body and the pull of gravity. What we call the weight of a body is simply the amount of pull of the earth's gravity on it so that the further away that body is from the earth, the less it will weigh because the earth does not pull it so hard.

Weight, as we know, is measured by scales in anything from milligrams to megatons, but as far as the human body and its movement is concerned (as well as the movement of certain animals), weight is not just a question of pounds, ounces or grams. We have all observed those miraculous fat people who move around with a tread as light as a feather, but where does the weight go? Conversely, we have witnessed thin people who stump about like guardsmen. Where has the weight come from? Perhaps the answer lies in Laban's observation that some people indulge in gravity and some resist it.

When athletes jump they are not judged by the lightness of their landing, though dancers certainly are, and it is interesting to compare how some dancers make less of a thud than others, and why. Some may achieve the desired result by intense training while others may do it by pure instinct but more important than technique is the preconception of the jump in the mind. Thus will the mind ensure the involvement of all the necessary muscles in a complete harmonious follow-through of movement. Even so, there have been some who seem to have been capable of using a sixth sense with regard to weight which further resisted the pull of gravity. An example is the fabled leap of the great dancer Nijinsky, who, eye-witnesses have assured us, could spring high into the air and seem to remain hovering motionless before descending soundlessly to the floor. Similarly, there is the example of the mother who defied weight and gravity by lifting a car off her child who had been knocked down by it and was lying under it. How did she do it? Did Nijinsky really hover in mid-air?

Weight, certainly as far as movement is concerned, can seriously affect our relationship with both space and time. If we ourselves are a heavy weight (or carrying a heavy weight) we can be weighed down and slowed up unless we are pushed or dropped from a height. Illness, drunkenness or staggering about aboard ship in stormy weather can cause the loss of balance, the result of unequal tension.

Moving the body anywhere in space requires energy along a light-to-strong continuum. Because the body senses how much force is needed for these different movements, it is called **kinetic force**. Sometimes the body appears 'static', as in holding a position. Even so, these 'static' positions require a sufficient degree of force and energy to maintain them.

Then there is the force we need to use against obstacles, be it an object or a person. A gentle push to a child requires much less force than trying to push a car that has run out of petrol. Both child and car offer external resistance, but in one, it is lightly overcome and in the other, greater energy is needed. In both cases, it is applied directly to the **external resistance**.

As for the sort of weight that we have to pick up and hold, that is a real test for our **kinetic sensing.** There is a tremendous difference in the amount of effort needed to pick up a sheet of notepaper or a pail of water.

The human race comes in all shapes and sizes, yet most people have no problem with standing on two feet. From the day they first stood up as toddlers they have acquired a suitable tension between their bodies and the pull of gravity. It is something we take for granted until the occasions when the 'normally' balanced tension between our bodies and the pull of gravity is disturbed, such as dizziness, fainting, drunkenness or trying to keep one's balance during an earthquake. As Laban said, the centre of gravity of the upright body is approximately where the intersections of the three-dimensional cross meet, making this point the centre of our kinesphere.

### Exercises to Demonstrate the Body's Weight and the Pull of Gravity

● 1a. Walk around the room with a feeling of well-being and be aware of a pleasant sensation in your centre as though you have just had a nice meal. You feel neither light nor heavy. All is well, you are happy and content and the possibility of falling over is out of the question.

● b. Imagine you can move your centre up and down like a ring on your finger: slide it up to the top, light area, and walk around the room with this new, high centre. Your walk will take on an exaggerated lightness, your heels barely touching the floor. In attempting to be much lighter than you are, your balance will be disturbed. Even your head and thinking becomes affected.

● c. Now imagine you have moved the ring down to the bottom of your finger, towards the strong area and walk around the room with this new, low centre. From this very deep point, somewhere below your knees, your walk will take on an exaggerated heaviness. Your weight will have increased dramatically, and you will require much more effort to move around the room whilst trying to remain upright. It will be hard to combat the pull of gravity and not sink to the floor. Your mind should also be heavy.

● d. In your imagination walk around the room once again but swiftly change your movement origin centres from 1b, high, to 1c, strong. The contrast, from a dizzy light-headedness and exaggeratedly light movement to being almost overcome by weighty heaviness, can disorientate the mind and body which can only be restored to a sense of well-being by a return to the 'normal' centre of the body (1a), which is recognised as the origin of harmonious movement.

The exercises 1b) and 1c) were clearly placed near the far ends of the weight continuum. Less extreme movement behaviour can be beneficial in many cases:-

● e. With 1b in mind, lift your centre of gravity to your chest level, giving you a lightly-held stance, with your weight a little forward on your toes, like a boxer (lightly anti-gravity).

● f. A heavy jump: jump with both feet onto something you wish to flatten. This is indulging in gravity.

● g. A light jump: jump as lightly as you can, making as little sound as possible. This may involve landing on one foot or two but certainly the ball of the foot would make the first contact with the ground. Imagine you are landing on a surface that might give way if you are too heavy or, like 007, you might get shot if you are heard!

h. The heavy dancing partner: this is ideal for two people, one of whom is a ballerina. The other is her partner who will lift her into the air. If the ballerina lifts her centre as she is lifted, she will seem gossamer light and her partner will have no difficulty in bearing her aloft!

However, if the ballerina does not lift her centre upwards and is heavy in mood, she will be a dead weight, to the dismay of her partner.

Try both ways, then, if you feel able, swap roles.

## *Exercises to Demonstrate the Body Carrying Weights: Kinetic Sensing*

● 2a. Pick up a sheet of notepaper; from previous experience, we know this requires minimal effort. Feel the weight of the paper and assess how much pressure you need to exert between your thumb and one or two fingers. If the pressure is too light the paper will slip from your fingers; if the pressure is too strong you stand the risk of bruising the paper and spoiling it.

● b. Picking up a pail of water requires a great deal more effort than a sheet of paper. Again, from past experience, our kinetic sense will anticipate how much effort to use. However, a pail of water may not be readily at hand, so look around you for something heavy that you can pick up with one hand. If you have not picked this object up before your kinetic sense may not anticipate the correct amount of effort needed, in which case you must find out when you lift it. It may be much heavier than you expected and you must exert greater strength. If it is lighter than you expected it will suddenly fly up.

● c. With one hand pick up a sheet of paper or something similarly light and in the other hand something really heavy. Compare the two sensations and whether they affect each other and check whether your pressure on the paper is too strong.

● d. Imagine that you work in a museum and your job is to dust very carefully the delicate porcelain treasures on display. Each piece is a different size and weight. Some of them are damaged and have to be handled with extra care. Size is not always related to weight, and delicate handles and spouts have to be taken into account, and so the right amount of energy (i.e. light, kinetic force) must be selected in each action.

● e. You can try this as an exercise or imagine it. Wearing a very heavy rucksack, the posture of your spine will be forced to incline forward to counterbalance the weight pulling you back.

● f. Another one to be imagined: you are carrying a weighty shoulder bag such as you see passengers carrying as hand baggage when boarding a plane. The shoulder that supports the strap will be grotesquely raised to cope with the weight and stop the strap sliding off. Doing this constantly can cause serious spinal problems.

● g. It is impressive to see how skilfully certain nationalities can carry baskets or pots on their heads without so much as wavering. Contrary to 2f, this is good for the spine and posture. This is partly due to the lifting of the weight-centre of the body upwards (as in Exercise 1b) to counteract the weight of the load. Apart from a few admirable market porters, the nearest we Westerners have got to this is in schools of deportment where girls walk round the room with books on their heads. The very thought of carrying something on your head should make your spine lengthen upwards, but in order to do so, you need to make a secure platform with a cap or twisted cloth. Then select something suitable to place on top – not a pail of water – but something light and unbreakable like a bundle of newspapers. Have fun. You may look daft, but it's wonderfully enlightening for the spine.

● h. In the laws of leverage, the heavier the weight to be lifted, the nearer the body lifting it, and that body's centre of gravity, needs to be to it, generating greater strength. For instance, if you try to lift a heavy object off the floor without flexing your knees you are liable to do yourself an injury. What kinetic sense without previous experience does not always tell us is how to lift a dead weight, such as a disabled person or a patient lying in bed, but any nurse with her training will tell you that the strain must be taken by the thigh muscles. Try this with an understanding partner. It could prove to be a very useful experience!

### Exercises to demonstrate body resistance:
### Pulling and Pushing

● 3a. Pushing a dead weight: brace yourself to push a really heavy piece of furniture, like a piano. You will notice that you automatic- ally stand close to it with your arms bent close to your body. Also, take note that you will take a deep breath which will be locked in by the epiglottis at the top of the windpipe to give you extra power to pitch your own weight against the heavy mass. This breath is only released when the piano moves or you give up because it won't move.

● b. Pushing against a dead weight that suddenly gives way: this is better tried with a person as pianos aren't so obliging. It is very like pushing against an obstinate door which suddenly opens and sends you flying into the room. Get a friend to stand firm while you try to push him out of the way. When he suddenly gives way, your own weight will precipitate you in the direction you are pushing, and you will suddenly breathe out.

c. Pulling a dead weight: Pulling a piano or heavy piece of furniture on one's own is likely to be as futile as pushing it. Here, your body weight will be used in the opposite direction to the object. Your arms will be more extended but nevertheless flexed with your elbows close to your body to muster all available strength from the body-centre. Again, you will take a deep breath and hold it while you pull.

d. Pulling a dead weight that suddenly gives way: this is something we have all done, sometimes to our cost. Leaning backwards, you could be tugging on a rope with all your might when it suddenly snaps, sending you and your complete body weight crashing to the floor, accompanied by a brisk exhalation. This can be quite fun if the surroundings are suitably soft.

e. Pushing something light with little resistance: an obvious example of this is walking along pushing a bicycle. Here the breathing will be easy and normal.

f. Pulling something light with little resistance: pulling a zip or curtains on easy runners.

g. Slamming a tennis ball with a racquet is a form of pushing, especially in the serve. Here the breath is very much part of the action. During the slow aim and preparation the breath is taken in and locked until the the racquet slams the ball when it is released, often causing an unpleasant strangulated cry.

h. Compare throwing and catching a ping-pong ball, which is ultra light, with throwing and catching a cricket ball, which is comparatively heavy. This is a good way to compare your kinetic sensing. Also, compare the difference in the breathing.

i. Imagine you are standing in an over-crowded train in the rush hour. This train is continually stopping and starting and throwing you off-balance so that you reach for support to keep upright. Light or strong anti-gravity exertion would be useless. Even a light, static exertion would not help. What is needed is a strong, kinetic force. Sense the direction and position to take up and when to adjust your balance. All this can occur in a very small area. When the motion of the train is smooth-running, your strong, kinetic force will diminish, becoming almost static. However, a sharp swerve throws you off-balance, and you must make a strong movement in order to regain it.

It is possible to hold a bodily position and counter-balance the gravitational pull, although these positions are not usually held for any length of time. Training in mind and body, as in some of the martial arts, assists the practitioner to overcome exhaustion, and he is able to sustain a held position for more than an hour.

● j. Imagine you are a weight-lifter lifting an enormous bar-bell. Getting it from the ground to above your head is a strenuous and wobbly business, but once the bar-bell is aloft you will find you can lock yourself into a 'held' position – a good example of strong, static tension. Strong static tension is often used in 'held' positions. Try the exercise with a heavy book in each hand.

● k. You are waiting for a friend who is late. You are looking forward to seeing him but you are also agitated because, if he doesn't turn up soon, you will have to hurry off to an important business meeting. Light static force would almost certainly be experienced as you wait expectantly using minimal tension and counter-tension.

● l. Light minimal force against outside resistance: you are curious to know whether the door you painted with high gloss paint is dry, so very carefully you place a finger lightly on it. If you press too hard and the paint is not dry, you will leave a mark.

● m. Imagine pushing a heavy roller over a bumpy lawn or cycling up a steep hill. Strong, energetic interaction against outside resistance can be seen in kicking a football, driving off at golf, pushing a car or banging angrily on the piano keys.

## FLOW

Flow is something we usually associate with liquid; the thinner the liquid is (such as water) the greater will be the flow. But water needs to be released from its inertia or state of rest and to respond to the pull of gravity (such as a downward slope) in order to flow. Flow describes movement which is unimpeded and continuous. Hair is sometimes described as flowing, as are certain robes and some types of handwriting. Where human movement is concerned, Laban considered the motion factor of flow as playing an important part in all movement expression, and that through its inward and outward streaming it establishes relationships and communication. Flow is mainly concerned with the degree of liberation in movement as, for example, the contrasts of being 'free in' or 'free from' the actual flow. To understand and describe flow it is nesessary to consider its complete opposite: movement which is broken up and jerky with the quality of 'starting and stopping'.

In bodily movement, flow can be successive or simultaneous. Successive flow occurs when one body part follows another, carrying the movement along. Simultaneous flow occurs when the whole body moves at the same time. However, it is possible to move both in a simultaneously flowing way and a successively flowing way. For example, a trunk movement can travel upwards from the knees, through the hips, chest, shoulders and head. These movements are often curved or undulating, i.e. related to the arcs and circles mentioned earlier. Successive flow in the adjacent parts of the arms and legs would be shoulders, elbows, wrists, hands and fingers and their reverse order, or hips, knees and feet and their reverse order. A successive movement backwards with the hips, knees and feet is not possible as the knees can only bend forward. Jerky or detached movements can also be successive or simultaneous, in which case the flow is interrupted.

### Free-Flow and Bound-Flow

Flow can be considered to be free when it is entirely unimpeded and difficult to stop suddenly. As with water flowing down a slope, the mover feels there are no problems; he is not expecting any errors, neither does he feel there is a need to adjust or change his mind. Confident, he sees no reason to put the action 'on hold'. There is a 'whole-heartedness' about this fluency of action. It is a confident approach as opposed to being diffident. But all actions are not confined to being either confident or diffident. Bound flow can be either tentative, as when stroking a dog that may bite you, or it can be confident, when you are performing a task that requires care but you know exactly what you are doing. The emotions are more than likely not involved – unless the dog bites!

**Contrasting free-flow with bound-flow**

● Two good examples are within the experience of most of us: when painting or whitewashing a wall, you will use a large brush and employ broad, sweeping strokes from the shoulder. This is an enjoyable movement with a feeling of freedom. Contrast this with painting the window frame where you employ a steady hand but are careful not to get any paint on the glass.

# 4

# *The Eight Basic Efforts*

| | |
|---|---|
| *Pressing* | *Slashing* |
| *Flicking* | *Gliding* |
| *Wringing* | *Thrusting* |
| *Dabbing* | *Floating* |

Every single human being has his or her personal characteristics and mannerisms of movement behaviour and speech patterns. Some may be pleasing to the eye or ear, others not, but there is no doubt that the course of civilisation has greatly reduced the potential of the magnificent machine that is the human body. Visits to gyms and health clubs are only partly successful in redressing this. True, exercise routines will be followed, and mind-numbing sessions will take place on cycles and treadmills, but it is doubtful whether all the muscles will be equally served; some will be overworked and others hardly used. There will be much puffing and blowing and a great deal of stress and strain.

Laban's conception involved a very different approach; in contrast to, say, a ballet training where most of the movements are remote from everyday life, Laban could envisage our natural potential and make us relish our freedom. Sometimes, he would make his students strive, but there would be no stress or strain, and at no time would the mind not be involved. He reduced the countless movements the human body is capable of making, down to eight basic efforts. These basic efforts we all do in various ways and degrees every day, though many of us tend to remain mostly in one or two effort areas and rarely venture into the others. We have all witnessed the person who floats through life and whose most energetic movement is a quick dab. Likewise, we have witnessed those who move like a bull in a china shop and who couldn't float or glide to save their lives. Laban takes his eight basic efforts and makes us experience each one to the full. However, as exercises, he sometimes placed them in unexpected parts of our kinesphere as we shall discover.

**Space** This motion factor consists of two elements, Direct and Flexible. The Direct element has a clearly defined movement in a straight line and is, therefore, said to be 'resisting' or 'fighting against' Space. The Flexible element consists of a wavy, multi-directional movement and is said to be 'yielding' or 'indulging' in Space.

**Time** This motion factor consists of two elements, Sudden and Sustained. The Sudden element consists of a quick speed and is said to be 'resisting' or 'fighting against' Time. The Sustained element consists of a slow speed and is said to be 'yielding' or 'indulging' in Time.

**Weight** This motion factor has two elements, Strong and Light. The Strong element consists of a firm resistance to Weight and is said to be 'resisting' or 'fighting against' Weight. The Light element consists of a weak, or relaxed, resistance to Weight and is said to be 'yielding' or 'indulging' in Weight.

**Pressing:
Direct, Sustained, Strong**

The word pressing brings to mind many movements and tasks that we perform daily. Some of the things we press require minimum pressure, such as door-bells, postage stamps onto envelopes, draw-ing pins into boards, buttons on equipment and poppers on clothes. Greater pressure is needed for ironing a crease into a pair of trousers or pushing a garden roller, whereas the pressure needed to push a piano, single handed, is almost superhuman. Pressing is closely allied to push-ing and crushing, also to squeezing which usually demands two oppos-ing pressures, as between finger and thumb, or an all-round pressure, as in a fist. However, as a *basic effort*, pressing is very strong, very direct and very sustained and is economical in the use of space. Pressing is a movement of obvious bound-flow. This means that the action can be halted on its spatial journey but is not entirely abandoned. Whilst the movement is controlled to the uttermost during this pause, a sensation of fluency remains. It is true we can press in almost any direction but some areas are more successful than others. For instance, pressing downwards is far more effective than pressing upwards because you have gravity and weight on your side.

### Exercises

● 1. Remind yourself of the sensation of heavy pressing by pitching your strength against a wall or immovable object. You might push forwards with both hands (your arms flexed close to your body for added strength) or you might press with one hand and the opposite shoulder, your whole body leaning obliquely towards the point of pressure, or you might push entirely with your back. Do not overdo this or strain yourself but, in each case, note the effect on your muscles.

● 2. Try pressing with other parts of your body such as your knees, your elbows, your feet and your head – even your nose.

● 3. Let two parts of the body press simultaneously in two different directions, for example, the palms of your hands pushing outwards.

● 4. Press simultaneously in three different directions, for example, head backward, hips forward and elbows outwards, away from their own sides.

● 5. Press down with the feet as they walk, taking the body in different directions.

● 6. Try pressing in kneeling, sitting and lying positions as well as standing.

● 7. Compare the isometric pressure (equally opposing) between thumb and forefinger with the isometric pressure of the heel of one hand against the heel of the other – a favourite exercise with athletes for strengthening the arms and pectoral muscles.

Try all these exercises out several times; it is important to 'get the feel' of the effort without any considerations of circumstances or (as in the case of the actor) of characterisation. In an everyday situation, one can push against a concrete object and feel its resistance, but when you are pressing or pushing against these objects in your imagination, you will find that you will use 'antagonistic muscle' groups to provide resistance. A counter-tension is set up in other parts of the body which will give you a feeling of controlled strength. Laban's use of the *basic effort* of pressing as a movement exercise requires a crossover movement, as follows:

● 8. Take a half step, crossing your right leg in front of your left; simultaneously, bring your right arm across your body and press the heel of your hand down towards the left, forward, deep corner of the cube. Let your body incline in the same direction without turning while the extended arm remains flexed for greater strength. Repeat the process, crossing from left to right.

The Pressing effort resists Weight and Space but indulges in Time

### Flicking: Flexible, Sudden, Light

Flicking is something we do quite frequently. We flick fluff off our clothes, flies off food and, sometimes, hair out of our eyes. Flicking is flexible in its use of space and it resists both Weight and Time. If the whole hand is used it is usually with the backs of the fingers making a backward, half-rotary motion. Flicking forwards or inwards with the fingers is more rare. A common form of flicking is to flick the middle finger off the thumb. It is, however, quite possible to flick with other parts of the body.

As a *basic effort*, flicking is a movement with obvious free flow; it is crisp and light and always brief and is quite unlike the action of relaxed shaking.

● 1. Remind yourself of the sensation of flicking, and flick a piece of imaginary (or real) fluff off your sleeve.

● 2. Repeat the same flicking movement all round yourself (a swarm of flies, perhaps) both near and far away from your body and reaching to the high, medium and deep zones. Make sure you reach high and low, backwards and forwards as well as both sides. Nevertheless, it is essential to try it in all directions, with the hands working simultaneously or alternately, in the same, or in different, directions.

● 3. Try flicking with your feet – not as easy as with the hands but sometimes necessary.

● 4. If you flick your feet rhythmically on the floor (forwards and back), you will probably have performed a 'shuffle', the basic step of tap dancing. You can even try jumping and flicking your feet in the air.

● 5. Continue the exploration of flicking with your elbows, your knees, your nose, your chin and unlikely parts like your hips and stomach.

● 6. Try repeated flicking as fast as you can so that it produces a flickering or fluttering movement. When the whole body becomes involved, there is a sense of lightness and buoyancy. Laban had a party trick of fluttering his hand so fast that a finger and thumb seemed to disappear.

These exercises will help you to develop a valuable effort control and will give an entirely different movement experience from, say, simple relaxing, shaking, exercises.

The Flicking effort is indulgent in Space and Weight but resists Time.

## Wringing: Flexible, Sustained, Strong

Wringing makes us think of wet clothes or a cloth that has to be wrung out. The most common occurrence, surely, in our daily lives is to wring out a wet face-flannel. However, as a basic effort, you need not only wring an imaginary wet cloth in your hands but can involve all parts of your body in the wringing effort. Wringing is closely related to twisting and primarily involves the hands moving in opposition to each other. From the hands the wringing movement can spread to the arms and then throughout the body.

● 1. Remind yourself of the sensation of wringing, in the hands first, as if wringing out a wet cloth.

● 2. Imagine you are a wet cloth being wrung out by somebody else! This will require some counter-tension on your part but try being wrung or twisting yourself in both directions. This is similar to many exercises in the gym.

● 3. Try wringing movements in all zones and in all directions of your kinesphere.

● 4. Having wrung your arms in opposition to each other, try wringing movements with each arm separately.

● 5. Extend your arms out sideways and wring them in opposite directions.

● 6. As well as sideways, wring your arms upwards and downwards, backwards and forwards, and across each other.

● 7. Wring your body in both directions.

● 8. Try wringing gestures with your legs such as a screwing motion with your foot on the floor as when smokers stub out a cigarette end.

● 9. Imagine your ankle is a wet sponge and wring it out.

There are many examples of wringing where there is concrete resistance by the object being wrung. Where no such concrete resistance exists and you are having to use your imagination, a strong counter-tension is necessary and can be felt throughout the body.

The Wringing effort is indulgent in Space and Time but resists Weight. It is usually performed with bound-flow.

## Dabbing:
## Direct, Sudden, Light

Dabbing is another light movement we perform fairly frequently. We dab computer keyboards, we make dabs with paint brushes, and we dab our eyes when we weep. As a *basic effort*, dabbing is direct, sudden and light  and is usually performed with free-flow which is very flexible and from which there is nearly always a rebound. Dabbing can also be performed with bound-flow. This is more difficult and is without much, if any, rebound and is more like poking. Try each exercise both ways. You can dab with the hands in all directions – upwards, downwards, forwards and backwards and sideways. You can also dab with your feet and other extremities of the body.

- 1. Remind yourself of the sensation of dabbing by imagining you have a paint brush, newly dipped in the paint, and that you are dabbing the colour on the walls, floor and ceiling of something like the cube. Whether you are left-handed or right, try both sides.

- 2. With your right hand try dabbing the left side of the cube, keeping your feet firmly placed and twisting (wringing) your body round to reach the back. Also, do a splendid back-bend to dab the ceiling. Repeat the process with your left hand.

- 3. Dab with your feet. Alternate with heel and toe, in all directions and in all zones, even lying on the floor to do so. A particularly pleasant sensation is to be seated and lift one foot slightly off the floor and to dab the toes sharply down, tapping the floor. This is a wonderful exercise for emphasising the flexibility of the ankles. Dabbing with the heel is not so easy or pleasing. Organists who play the pedals will sympathise here.

- 4. Dab with your knees, hips, shoulders, back, chest, elbows, head, chin, and your nose. Take plenty of time to experience dabbing in all parts of the body. Some parts will lend themselves more readily to the effort than others but do persevere with the more awkward areas like your back or chest. Remember that you are trying to extend your range of movement.

- 5. Try the action with steps. Knees can dab upwards and toes or heels downwards. When dabbing at a tangible object, such as a computer keyboard, we experience some resistance. However, dabbing in the air requires muscles to produce the necessary counter-tension which can be felt throughout the body even if only one finger is involved in the action.

The Dabbing effort indulges in Weight but resists Time and Space

## Slashing:
## Sudden, Strong, Flexible

Slashing is not a movement we perform often unless we are involved in combat or play tennis. We associate the movement with bringing a sword or some such weapon swiftly down diagonally so as to cut a swathe in whatever is in front – we have seen it so many times in films.

Slashing a painting is another familiar image (remember the suffragette who slashed Velasquez's *Rokeby Venus* because it glorified a woman in the nude) but is a more deft and flexible movement. Whipping is similar but not quite so violent. Beating is also a similar movement but is more rigid. As a *basic effort*, slashing is sudden, strong, swift and flexible. It is usually performed with free-flow which tends to diminish into floating which can remain bound or remain free. Slashing aimed at a tangible object encounters resistance. The great freedom of this action in the air, is that it requires various muscle groups to provide strong counter-tension.

- 1. Try the most obvious movement of slashing – bringing a sword down on an assailant in front of you. If you are right-handed you will naturally use your right arm, which will be raised high behind your right shoulder. With lightning speed bring your fist holding the sword diagonally down across your body. If you imagine the assailant receiving this blow, your arm will suddenly stop directly in front of you, in which case note how some of your muscles that were indulging in free flow will go into counter-tension. On the other hand, if you are so strong that your sword cuts through the poor fellow like butter, your slashing movement will diminish in strength and speed until it comes to rest right across your body. Repeat with your other arm.

- 2. Try the arms slashing separately in all directions.

- 3. Instead of performing one slashing movement at a time, try several in a continuous zig-zag movement. This is much more flexible and should develop into a figure-of-eight movement with your arm going well behind you and well in front of you.

- 4. Now try slashing with each leg separately and then your feet.

- 5. Continue slashing with your limbs separately or together, kneeling, sitting, lying or standing; all directions including inwards and outwards and moving in different zones.

- 6. Try slashing movements with your body, starting with your shoulders, but don't overdo it!

- 7. Large jumps give good opportunities for slashing movements of the legs, arms and trunk.

The Slashing effort indulges in Space, but resists Time and Weight.

## Gliding: Sustained, Light, Direct

Gliding is essentially a smooth movement such as we observe in ice-skating and glider planes. As far as the human body is concerned, we tend to associate gliding with our feet, either sliding them along the floor or moving them in such a way that we seem to be gliding. However, gliding can easily be felt with the palms of the hands or fingertips as when feeling silk or stroking a cat. As a *basic effort*, gliding is sustained, light and direct and is usually performed with bound flow. When gliding along a tangible surface there is a small amount of resistance but when performing the same movement in the air there are certain muscular counter-tensions which supply the feeling of controlled or bound flow.

- 1. Run the palms of your hands over a smooth horizontal surface. Probably, you will start with your hands close together and move them outwards which would certainly be the case if you were stroking a cloth. Try to analyse the activity of your muscles governing the movement and then repeat the same action in the air.

- 2. Do a vertical gliding movement with the palm of one hand then the other as though sliding it down a smooth wall or marble pillar.

137

● 3. Try gliding movements with your hands in all directions round your body, each hand separately or both together. Glide upwards and downwards, backwards and forwards and from side to side, using all the zones.

● 4. Glide with your feet so that you move smoothly across the room.

● 5. Connect gliding feet with gliding gestures.

● 6. Glide with various parts of your body. The hips can glide in a circle, so can the shoulders. Try them together in opposite directions – a very good exercise for potential belly-dancers!

The Gliding effort indulges in Weight and Time, but resists Space.

### Thrusting or Punching: Direct, Sudden, Strong

Both punching and thrusting are violent, direct movements and can be performed with bound or free flow. The most familiar form of punching is the clenched fist thrusting vehemently at a target. When punching the air, rather than a target, the counter-tension of the antagonistic muscles will be strongly felt. As a *basic effort,* punching is direct, sudden and strong and its essential characteristics involve overcoming Weight, Space and Time, therefore, there is no indulgence in this action, no yielding to lightness or flexibility and no yielding to sustainment of the movement.

● 1. With one arm at a time and a clenched fist, punch in all directions round your body.

● 2. Punch the floor with your feet, which is like stamping, then punch the air with your feet in as many directions as you can manage.

● 3. Punch the air with your elbows and then with your knees. Be daring and punch with one elbow and the opposite knee.

● 4. Punch the air with your shoulders, in different directions but not too violently, and then punch with your hips (a touch of 'bump and grind' here).

● 5. You can try punching with your head but exercise caution here to avoid dislocating your neck. The safest direction is forwards as in the 'head-butt', a movement used by thugs to break somebody's nose – not pleasant.

● 6. Explore your kinesphere in all directions and zones, using the parts of the body simultaneously or alternately. One doesn't need to remain standing. It is possible to punch in a kneeling, sitting or lying position. For instance, lie down on your back and punch the air with your feet as far as you can reach, even lifting your hips off the ground.

The Thrusting effort resists Time, Weight and Space.

## Floating: Flexible, Sustained, Light

Floating is similar to flying and can be performed with bound or free flow. Floating can either be through the air or on water. We can float our bodies on water but not through the air without some aid such as a para- chute. However, we can float  our arms and we can seem to float when we walk. Floating suggests buoyancy and weightlessness, and in this it differs from gliding. As a *basic effort*, floating is flexible, sustained and light. It is also slow and tends to lack direction, sometimes to the point of aimlessness. Some- times we float in our dreams and in a state of half-wakefulness. Floating develops an invaluable effort control that is quite different from doing exercises of simple, slow movements. The slight and multi-lateral counter-tensions produce a special kind of gentle sustainment which is different from any other physical action.

Floating movements can be performed in all the various zones.

● 1. Try floating each arm separately away from the body. Feel the lightness of your arm almost as though it is being inflated. In fact, the motion of breathing in very much helps the feeling of floating.

● 2. Float both arms together, symmetrically, like wings, then in contrary directions. Always, the feeling should be pleasant.

● 3. Try floating your head off your shoulders. As the head is actually very heavy, this is very beneficial to do.

● 4. Follow the floating of your head with floating shoulders and chest and extend this into a pleasing floating walk.

● 5. Float one leg, then the other, off the ground in various directions – make sure it feels light. (It may be advisable to hold onto a chair while you do this.)

● 6. Lie on the floor and let yourself relax. Float one arm off the floor, then the other, breathing in as you do so. Float one leg off the floor, then the other, remembering to breathe in. Float arms and legs off the floor in various pairings or all at once, even letting your head float up a little.

● 7. Finally, while you are still on the floor, feel that your body is so light that it is able to float upwards and thus, very slowly, rise to a standing position. You should feel glorious!

The Floating effort indulges in Space, Time and Weight.

Few actions in everyday life are limited to one basic effort. It is probable that at least two or even three efforts will be required to accomplish a task successfully. For instance, in heaving a heavy object onto a high shelf, you might swing it up in a slashing movement to be followed by a pressing movement to push the object further onto the shelf. There is also the question of how we prefer to move, which could well be linked to our personality. People are free to choose what they consider to be the most appropriate movements to complete a task, movements which will suit their personality. Those who prefer using light, sustained efforts will not be natural candidates for strong, sudden efforts, but with Laban's movement training the opportunity is there to extend their movement range to accomplish a wide variety of tasks successfully but without necessarily losing their individual preference. Efforts can be appropriate or inappropriate to the task in hand, or to the person performing the task, or both. These efforts can be performed with or without stressing the Flow factor which can also add to the appropriateness or inappropriateness of the effort being used to accomplish the task. It is essential to learn to control the flow factor in order to be able to use free flow and bound flow as and when necessary.

## THE DYNAMOSPHERE

The dynamosphere was Laban's term for the imaginary structure or three-dimensional chart which shows the dynamics of the eight *basic efforts* and their relationship to each other within the kinesphere, which is our movement globe. As you can see from the diagram below, the dimensional cross is placed in the centre of the cube (which we are viewing from behind) and each extremity of its three continuums coincides with the centre of each of the cube's six planes.

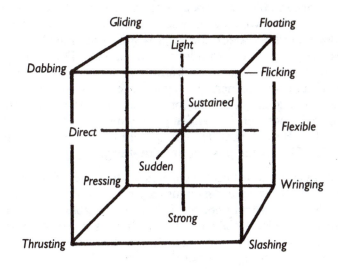

Figure 48: The Dimensional Cross within the Cube

We can see that the Weight continuum, from Light to Strong (or heavy), goes from the centre of the ceiling to the centre of the floor, indicating that Light is high while Strong is deep. The Space continuum, from Flexible to Direct, goes from the centre of one side of the cube to the centre of the other side. Why Flexible to Direct? This refers to the fact that if you move your right arm or leg on the right side, it has the freedom to be Flexible, but if you cross your right arm or leg across yourself towards the left wall, the movement is severely limited, is no longer Flexible and is, of necessity, Direct. The same goes for leading the movement with your left arm – the left side will be Flexible and the right side will be Direct. The Time continuum, from Sustained to Sudden, goes from the centre of the front wall to the centre of the back wall. Why Sustained and why Sudden? Laban quite rightly observed that we use our legs and arms, particularly our arms, mostly in front of our bodies where the movement is easily sustainable, but any movement of our limbs performed behind our body is of necessity short, and therefore Sudden.

### Discovering the Eight Basic Efforts

- First of all, take the four top corners of the cube which are in the Light area. Using your right arm, lift it towards the High/Right, front corner. Here, you are able to move in the Light, Flexible, Sustained area, which gives rise to **Floating**. If you move your arm to the Right/High/Back corner, it is still in the Flexible and Light area but the position is no longer Sustainable. This is the position for **Flicking**. Now move the same arm across your body to the Left/High/Front corner. Here, your arm is still in the Light and Sustainable area but it is no longer Flexible and is therefore Direct. This is the position for **Gliding**. Now move your arm towards the Left/High/Back corner. Here it is Light but not Sustainable or Flexible. This is the position for **Dabbing**.

- Next, take the four bottom corners of the cube, which are in the Strong, or heavy, area. Again, using your right arm, move it towards the Right/Deep/Front corner. Here, you are able to move in the Strong, Flexible, Sustained area, which gives rise to **Wringing**. If you move your arm to the Right/Deep/Back corner, it is still in the Flexible and Strong area but the position is no longer Sustainable. This is the position for **Slashing**. Now move your right arm across your body to the Left/Deep/Front corner. Here, your arm is still in the Strong, Sustainable area but is no longer Flexible and is therefore Direct. This is the position for **Thrusting**. Finally, move your right arm to the Left/Deep/Back corner. Here it is Strong and Direct but not sustainable. This is the position for **Pressing**.

We have seen how the three continuums of the Dimensional Cross provide a logical location for each of the eight basic efforts in the eight corners of the cube, but it is fair to say that any of the efforts can be performed with varying degrees of success in any part of the kinesphere. However, to reinforce the logic of the positions it is useful to compare the diagonally opposite corners.

- Leading from the left side, this time take your left arm up to the Left/High/Forward corner (**Floating**) before crossing your body with it and reaching towards the Right/Deep/Back corner (**Thrusting**). The contrast between the opposites of Floating and Thrusting can be clearly felt. Now, take your left arm up to the Right/High/Front corner (**Gliding**) and bring it down to the Left/Deep/Back corner (**Slashing**). Feel the contrast of opposites. Next, take your left arm up to the Left/High/Back corner (**Flicking**) and swoop down to the Right/Deep/Front corner (**Pressing**) and feel the contrast. Lastly, raise your left arm across to the Right/High/Back corner (**Dabbing**) before taking it down to the Left/Deep/Front corner (**Wringing**) and feel the contrast. Indeed, all the contrasts should be self-evident. You may wonder whether experiencing the eight basic efforts in the dynamosphere is confined to the arms and can it be done with the legs. Well, Laban would probably say, try it. Your success would be limited but at least you can say you have tried!

### Changing one element

Involving Adjacent Effort Corners.

● Let us now look more specifically at the relationship of one effort to another. The corners will now be referred to by their initials only e.g. Right/High/Front will be R/H/F.

Moving from one adjacent corner to another changes only one element and thus facilitates an easy effort transition. For example:

● With your right arm move to the R/H/F corner , the position for Floating. From this corner move your arm across to the L/H/F corner , the position for Gliding. Both efforts, as we know, are at the same end of the Weight continuum, which is Light. The action goes from a Flexible to a Direct movement and vice versa. If your right arm moves from the L/H/F corner towards the L/D/F corner , the position for Pressing, this would mean only changing the Weight element and would mean another easy transition, this time from Gliding to Pressing. Try the reverse movement before continuing the pathway. From the new L/D/F corner 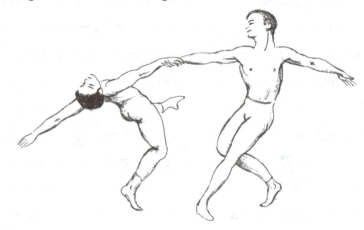 move your arm along to the R/D/F , the position for Wringing. This has been a spatial change only, from Direct to Flexible. (You may remember that a spatial change occurred when you moved from Floating to Gliding). Try the movement in reverse. Finally, move from the R/D/F corner up to the R/H/F corner , the position for Floating, your original starting position. Only the Weight continuum has changed from Strong to Light. Try the action in reverse. (The change here is similar to the change between Gliding and Pressing.)

- Try the sequence leading with the left side.

- The pathway can also be done in reverse order on the right and left sides. If you feel confident, make a little movement or dance sequence by taking steps and travelling in the right and left directions, even going on to your toes for the High corners and bending the knees a little in the Deep corners.

- The front plane or wall has been explored. Now explore for yourselves the Right, Back and Left planes. Remember to try the movements in reverse. After going through the pathway with your left side, enjoy travelling with a few steps which could go right to left (as in our example) or forward and backward, whilst either rising on the toes or sinking.

## Changes involving one element

|  | Changing Time | Changing Weight | Changing Space |
|---|---|---|---|
| *Float* | Flick | Wring | Glide |
| *Thrust* | Press | Dab | Slash |
| *Glide* | Dab | Press | Float |
| *Slash* | Wring | Flick | Thrust |
| *Dab* | Glide | Thrust | Flick |
| *Wring* | Slash | Float | Press |
| *Flick* | Float | Slash | Dab |
| *Press* | Thrust | Glide | Wring |

## Changing two elements

The table overleaf shows how, by changing two elements, the resulting basic effort is much more pronounced in contrast. For instance, in Floating (Sustained, Light and Flexible), when Weight and Time change, becoming Strong and Sudden, but Space remains Flexible, the basic effort becomes Slashing. When the Time and Space elements change to Sudden and Direct, and the Weight element remains Light, the basic effort becomes a Dab. When the Space and Weight elements change to Direct and Strong but the Time element remains sustained, the basic effort becomes Pressing. You will notice that Slashing, Dabbing and Pressing are in the next-but-one corners to Floating. In each case, the change in rhythm and expressive movement quality is also more pronounced. By-passing an adjacent corner and moving to the next-but-one effort corner is a rather more complicated change in movement quality.

● 1) Supposing your right arm is in the L/D/F corner █ , the position for Pressing, and you move it to Dabbing in the L/H/B corner ▨ , the only continuum remaining unchanged would be Space. The movement would remain direct but the Weight and Time elements would have changed. Try the movement in reverse order. As you practise, notice the changes in Weight and Time, from Sustained and Strong to Sudden and Light and vice versa. Both efforts remain direct in Space.

2) From the L/D/F corner █ , the position for Pressing, move your right arm to the R/D/B corner ◣ , the position for Slashing.

Both Space and Time continuums have changed whilst the Weight continuum remains Strong. Try the movement in reverse. Note expressive changes in the two efforts. Sustained and Direct have become Sudden and Flexible but strength has been maintained. Repeat on the left side.

Try adding steps and being aware of the changes in Time and Space whilst maintaining Strong.

|  | Changing Weight-Time. | Changing Time-Space | Changing Space-Weight |
|---|---|---|---|
| Float | Slash | Dab | Press |
| Thrust | Glide | Wring | Flick |
| Glide | Thrust | Flick | Wring |
| Slash | Float | Press | Dab |
| Dab | Press | Float | Slash |
| Wring | Flick | Thrust | Glide |
| Flick | Wring | Glide | Thrust |
| Press | Dab | Slash | Float |

● 3) From our starting corner L/D/F ▮ again, the position for Pressing, move your arm to the R/H/F corner ▨ , the position for Floating. The Time continuum remains sustainable but both Weight and Space have changed. Try the movement in reverse. Note the change from Direct and Strong to Flexible and Light whilst maintaining the sustained quality of the Time continuum. Try the sequence through with the left side leading.

● 4) As with the other movement sequences, try taking a few steps, rising on your toes or lowering the body a little, then try to work through the rest of the two-continuum changes for yourself, for example, Glide could move to Flick, Wring and Thrust.

## Changing three elements

● Leading from the left side, this time, take your left arm up to the L/H/F corner ▨ (Floating), before crossing your body with it and reaching towards the R/D/B corner ▮ (Thrusting). The contrast between the opposites of Floating and Thrusting can be clearly felt. Now, take your left arm up to the R/H/F corner ▨ (Gliding), and bring it down to the L/D/B corner ▮ (Slashing). Feel the contrast of opposites. Next, take your left arm up to the R/H/B corner ▨ (Dabbing), and swoop down to the L/D/F corner ▮ (Wringing), and feel the contrast. Lastly, raise your left arm across to the L/H/B corner ▨ (Flicking), and swoop to the R/D/F corner ▮ (Pressing) and feel the contrast. Indeed, all the contrasts should be self-evident.

● Try the changes in reverse order then repeat for the right side.

● Now take a few steps in the appropriate direction each time, forward or backward, slightly left or right, rising on your toes or lowering your body slightly and increasing and decreasing your speed. All the contrasts should be self-evident.

Float to Thrust. Alternatively, Thrust to Float.

Glide to Slash. Alternatively, Slash to Glide.

Dab to Wring. Alternatively, Wring to Dab.

Flick to Press. Alternatively, Press to Flick.

The basic efforts last for very short moments in time, seconds, maybe a little longer, but they are always changing. Sometimes a continuum may be stressed a little more or a little less than the other two. (Later we will see how one continuum can be replaced altogether.)

The advantage of the dynamosphere diagram is that it is a visual aid showing the relationship of all the eight basic efforts. Whilst Laban advocates practising the efforts in their own corners he also said they must then be practised all over the kinesphere; one doesn't have to stay in a certain corner for a particular effort since this would be inappropriate in everyday life.

Lastly, let us consider diagonally opposite efforts which change all three elements and therefore their movement qualities. It is possible to use these diagonals as an **Efforts Scale**.

## THE EFFORT SCALE

**Effort Scale for the Right Side**

Remember to remain facing forward throughout.

● Begin at stance. Leading with the right side, step to the R/F corner whilst your right arm floats into the R/H/F corner ◩ . Rise on to the demi-pointe if you can. Your left arm and leg are in counter-tension. Now transfer your weight over your left foot as your right foot crosses behind your left leg and your right knee kneels in L/D/B ◗ . Your right arm simultaneously thrusts across the front of your body into the same direction, L/D/B ◗ . On rising, your right foot moves across in front of your body to the

148

L/F corner, on the demi-pointe if possible, as your right arm glides into the L/H/F direction . Your left arm and leg are in counter-tension. Now transfer your weight onto your left foot before stepping towards the open R/B corner. Your right arm simultaneously slashing towards this corner (R/D/B) . Your left arm and leg again in counter-tension. Transfer your weight momentarily onto your left foot as your right foot crosses behind your body to the L/B corner. Rise on to the demi-pointe if possible. Simultaneously, your right arm crosses in front of your body, dabbing into the same L/H/B corner . Your left arm and leg are crossed in counter-tension. Again, momentarily transferring your weight to your slightly raised left leg, step towards the R/F corner whilst wringing with your right arm in the same direction (R/D/F) . Your left arm and leg are in counter-tension. Finally, after transferring your weight, your right foot steps into the R/B corner, on the demi-pointe, if possible, as your right arm flicks into the same R/H/B corner . Your left arm and leg are in counter-tension. Briefly transferring your weight onto your left foot, step with your right foot into the L/F corner whilst pressing with your right arm into the same corner (L/D/F) . Your left arm and leg are in counter-tension behind your body. Repeat with the left side leading.

## THE EFFORT GRAPH

The effort graph came about because little was known about the relationship between exertion and control in any activity and, therefore, without scientific study, no real terminology existed which could be used to describe this relationship in a clear and precise manner. Laban called the effort graph 'a simple device' to record and evaluate any action and the effort content of that action within the four motion factors of Space, Time, Weight and Flow. It is an invaluable form of shorthand for those engaged in categorizing the effort used in movements, such as anthropologists comparing the movement characteristics of various tribes and races, time-and-motion specialists who need to make quick notes and, indeed, anyone who needs to assess the effort in movement and whether it is appropriate to the task. The effort graph is based on the simple device of a horizontal line crossing a vertical line at right angles. This should not be confused with the Dimensional Cross in spite of the fact that the vertical line also represents the continuum of Weight. Here, the horizontal line represents the continuum of Flow.

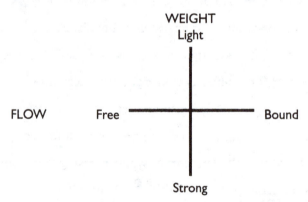

Figure 49 : The Effort Graph showing Weight and Flow

Unlike the Dimensional Cross, the effort graph is not three-dimensional and the left and right sides do not indicate the left and right sides of the body. The vertical line, representing Weight, runs from Light at the top to Strong or Heavy at the bottom. (The overall description of any movement can be called exertion.) The horizontal line, representing Flow, runs from Free Flow on the left to Bound Flow on the right. This simple cross is able to show us the four combinations of Weight and Flow.

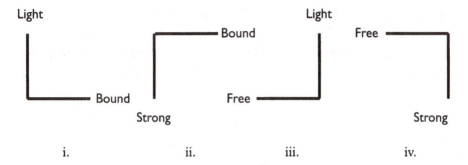

i.                    ii.                    iii.                    iv.

These four right angles refer to the Weight and Flow motion factors only. In *i*, the Light end of the Weight motion factor is indicated, so we know the movement is Light. The horizontal line is on the right side of the Flow motion factor, indicating Bound Flow. A Light action using Bound Flow is indicated and would be appropriate for, say, carrying a precious object. In *ii*, the Weight motion factor has changed to Heavy (Strong) but the Flow motion factor remains Bound. The action is now Heavy (Strong) with Bound Flow. This combination would not be suitable for carrying something light as in *i*, but would be perfectly appropriate for moving a heavy object such as a grand piano into position. In *iii*, both motion factors have changed to their opposites, to Light on Weight and to Free-Flow on the Flow motion factor. Using a Light, Free movement would be completely inappropriate for both *i* and *ii*. In the former there would be a danger of dropping the precious object and in the latter, a Light and Free action is of little use in shifting a piano. Swinging a light object freely (accommodating your movement to the swinging motion) would be more suitable. Finally, in *iv*, the Flow motion factor again indicates Free-Flow but the Weight motion factor has returned to Heavy (Strong). Free-Flow and Heavy (Strong) exertion would be excellent when swinging or throwing heavy objects like ropes, say, from ship to shore, or in a gymnasium, in vaulting over a series of hurdles. In this 'simple device', we have worked through four combinations of the cross representing Weight and Flow.

To this cross must now be added signs that indicate the Space used in the effort and the Time taken. Space is represented in the top right-hand quarter of the cross by two lines meeting at right-angles. The vertical line of this (parallel to the top half of the Weight motion factor) indicates the Flexible end of the Space motion factor while the horizontal line

(parallel to the right side of the Flow motion factor) indicates Directness. The diagonal line that links the corner of the Space right-angle to
the junction of the Weight and Flow cross represents Effort and helps to
identify the relationship between Weight and Flow and Space.

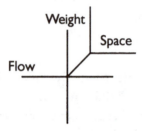

Figure 50: The Effort Graph minus the Time Factor

The appropriate effort graph (now including the Space motion factor)
for carrying a precious object would probably be Direct as in:

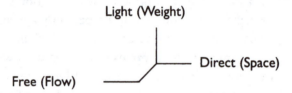

Directness in Space would also apply when moving a heavy object as in:

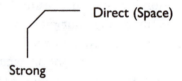

Whether the swinging object is light or heavy, when accompanied by
Free-Flow, the spatial pathway is Flexible.

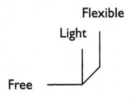

In order to complete the effort graph it only remains to add the indication of Time which appears as two short lines under and parallel to the Flow motion factor. The line on the left indicates Slow and Sustained movement while the one on the right represents Quick and Sudden movement.

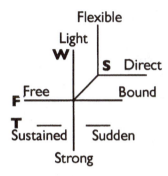

Figure 51: The Complete Effort Graph showing the Time Factor

The final exertion factor, that of Time, must be considered when taking any action. A movement can be too quick or too slow and thus mar an action which otherwise appears to be moderately efficient. Speed in the workplace is not always advisable even though it is often looked upon favourably. Similarly, in actions requiring caution, speed would be quite inappropriate and possibly dangerous. Dancers, working with an orchestra, are usually given steps by the choreographer which are appropriate to the speed and the rhythm of the music but, if there should be a different conductor one night who takes the music at double the speed, the result would be a shambles. So Time is a vital part of any effort. Some efforts simply cannot be efficiently achieved at too high a speed while other efforts cannot be sustained if the effort is too slow. We soon learn how fast a bicycle needs to go in order to stay upright, just as we learn through exercise and understanding that the proportion of Weight, Flow, Space and Time to each other is extremely important to any activity.

Using the effort graph, the eight basic efforts can be written as follows:

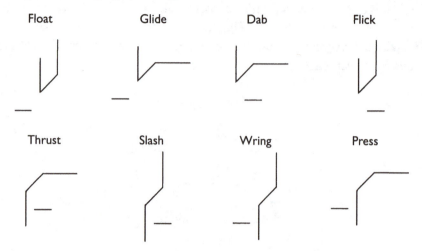

You will notice the absence of the Flow factor in the above signs. This is because in a routine movement, the Flow factor is neutral and therefore omitted. However, when feelings are involved, Flow, either bound or free, is of paramount importance as we shall see in the Incomplete Efforts.

We are now aware of how efforts can be appropriate or inappropriate to the task in hand but we have not considered whether or not the selected efforts were appropriate or inappropriate to the person carrying out the task. Whilst it is possible for people, either consciously or instinctively, to adapt and change efforts when necessary, to continue to do this over a long period could be detrimental to a person's health and well-being.

**Effort Variations: Ranks and Grades**

**Ranks**

A basic effort can be stressed by adding a dot (•). In this case, the moving person concentrates on one particular element, ranking it more important than the others which have become of secondary importance. For example, in an action requiring precise directness, the Space element would be stressed, ranking it as the most important element. In the Table opposite, the most appropriate word has been chosen to accompany the stressed element.

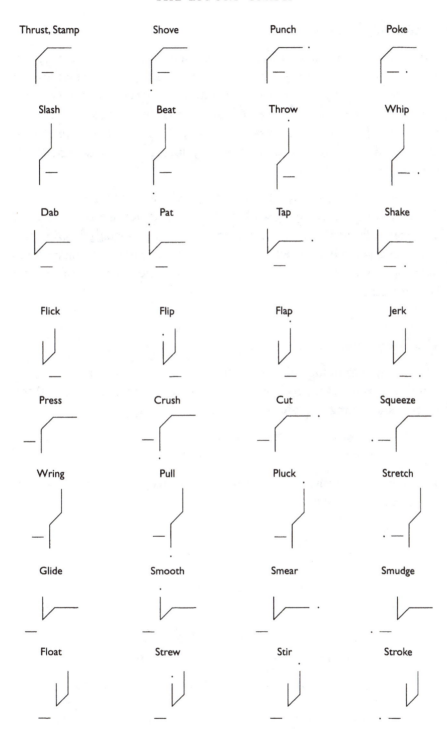

Thrust, Stamp   Shove   Punch   Poke

Slash   Beat   Throw   Whip

Dab   Pat   Tap   Shake

Flick   Flip   Flap   Jerk

Press   Crush   Cut   Squeeze

Wring   Pull   Pluck   Stretch

Glide   Smooth   Smear   Smudge

Float   Strew   Stir   Stroke

## Grades of Intensity

Grades of intensity arise when the mover adapts his action to continue to work efficiently at a practical task. For example, it may be necessary to stress the Strong element when operating machinery whilst increasing the intensity of the Flexible element and, simultaneously, decreasing the Sustained element. It is also possible to apply the ranks and grades of intensity to symbolic gestures or, similarly, incorporate Flow to heighten expression.

Whilst it is possible to alter the elements, it is essential to find the appropriate grades of intensity to work efficiently, whether one is performing practical tasks, acting, dancing or miming. Extremely exaggerated intensity or exaggerately reduced grades make for distortion, leading to complete rigidity of the muscles or complete sloppiness resulting from the lack of tension.

## The Four Grades of Intensity

The four grades of intensity are 1) 'normal', 2) one element changing to a plus or a minus, 3) two elements changing to a plus or minus, 4) three elements changing to a plus or a minus.

More than normal intensity is shown as '+'.
Less than normal intensity is shown as '−'.

The reduced intensity sign is written horizontally or vertically for easy recognition. Example:

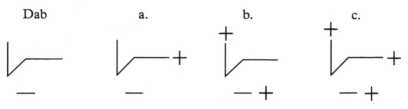

a. Direct intensity only increased.

b. Light and Sudden elements increased

c. Light, Sudden and Direct elements all increased in intensity.

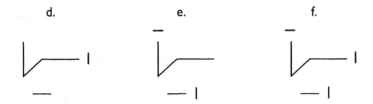

d. Direct intensity only reduced.

e. Light and Sudden elements decreased.

f. Light, Sudden and Direct elements all reduced in intensity.

Any one, two, or all three of the above elements have a different intensity. The wide range moves from reduced, normal, exaggerated to an extreme degree. The examples *a* to *c* may not be suitable for practical purposes but could heighten the expressive quality of the dancer or actor. The reduced intensity examples *d*, *e* and *f* give rise to further behaviour possibilities. Extreme exertion, or extreme relaxation due to reduced intensity can prevent a person achieving his objective.

It is possible for graded ranks to occur in combination.

Example: Pat

In the above instance, the light element is stressed but the elements of directness and suddenness are reduced, the action has a more lingering touch.

It is possible to maintain a stress on a particular element whilst also grading it:

Example: Tap

157

The stress on the direct element has now been joined by exaggerated intensity. It may be that this person is extremely exacting in his behaviour.

Finally, it is possible to indicate increasing and decreasing the gradings of the effort elements, making them more gradual in effect. The sign < denotes 'crescendo' (to increase), and > denotes 'decrescendo' (to decrease), as symbols in the effort graph. They refer to the grades only and do not change the character of the element where they appear. For example:

This person's attitude becomes more fixed the longer he continues his action.

## Shadow Movements

To distinguish a shadow movement from an operational one on the effort graph, the small diagonal line in the centre of the graph indicating the presence of effort, is crossed by a small stroke.

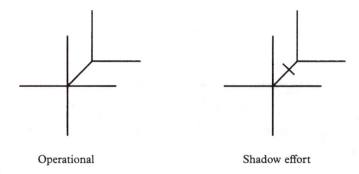

Operational                    Shadow effort

Shadow movements have always existed in human behaviour (and possibly animal behaviour, as well), but it was Laban who first drew our attention to them and gave them that name. They are the small, involuntary movements we make without being aware that we are making them, and are part of our body language – a shadowy part, it could be said – that can be extraordinarily revealing in a way that we might not welcome. They are the movements that we don't mean to make. A person might move and speak well, presenting himself with poise and confidence, using behavioural patterns that have been practised and are consciously made, but his shadow movements, that are not practised or consciously made, may tell a different story and reveal the real person behind the façade.

Shadow movements are discharges of inner tensions and are rarely, if ever, repetitive. They are completely spontaneous and are 'one-offs'; when they become repetitive or habitual, they can be recognised as mannerisms or just plain fidgeting. Much of personal human movement is accompanied by shadow movements. Usually small movements or gestures, they can occur at any time, either before or after a basic action or even accompanying it. The most common ones manifest themselves through the fingers, touching parts of the body or face. How often have we seen people being interviewed on television who, for no reason or useful purpose, suddenly rub their noses? Sometimes clothes are tugged at or hair is twirled, arms are crossed and uncrossed, necks twitch and jerk, bodies shift uneasily, as do legs and feet, all implying some sort of uneasiness. Mouths and eyebrows are great performers of shadow movements and can say a great deal about their owners.

The ability to assess character from shadow movements is invaluable when interviewing someone for a job. The hapless applicant may sit before you all scrubbed and groomed and eager to impress, but what is he doing with his fingers while you are questioning him? What is he doing with his feet? Must he fiddle with his shirt cuffs or mangle his tie? Does that twitch of his nose denote a sensitive nature or an arrogant attitude? It must be remembered that shadow movements can just as easily reveal pleasant or unpleasant traits in a person's character and there is comfort to be found in Laban's assessment that the person who displays a variety of shadow movements has imagination, whereas a person without any shadow movements is lacking in imagination!

## Conventional gestures

Convential gestures also occur in our everyday lives, usually as incomplete efforts unless an occasion of extreme excitement arises when a full basic action will appear, such as a slash or thrust. Nodding, winking, pointing and waving which replace words such as, 'OK', 'Here', 'Over there', 'Goodbye' are all conventional gestures.

For the actor, in particular, an understanding of incomplete effort actions, including shadow movements, is invaluable. Often the conscious selection of shadow movements for the role he or she is playing, will enhance the character. The inner attitudes heighten our mood, thus encouraging more expressive movement behaviour.

All human movement, whether it be unconscious shadow movements, conventional gestures, deliberate operational or functional actions (with all their stresses, gradings and ranking) can appear simultaneously or separately during any activity. They are mixed up in a most complex manner in human behaviour.

## The Effect of Feelings on Movement

Laban taught us to observe people and analyse their movement, which is an absorbing and fascinating occupation. In fact, we all do it to a greater or lesser degree when we sit on pavement cafés and 'people watch'. The shapes people create when moving are the results of chosen rhythmic pathways and reflect their moods. People's behaviour depends on one of two mental states as they go about their daily lives. These two mental states Laban called a) **Objective Function** and b) **Movement Sensation.** Both are present in all our movement activities but when one is active, the other remains passive or dormant.

## Objective Function

**Objective Function** is Laban's term for movements that are purely functional and that make no demands on our feelings or emotions. We hear people talk about being so familiar with a task that they can 'do it in their sleep'. This is because the necessary movements have become automatic. We witness and, indeed, perform such movements every day. Obvious examples are: getting dressed in the morning, cleaning one's teeth, even eating breakfast. With constant repetition, these activities have become purely routine and can be done without thinking, or we can do them whilst thinking about something else. Witness the shop-assistant who demonstrates how easy it is to pack up your purchases whilst gazing nonchalantly out of the window or gossiping to a colleague. People buffing their nails usually pay little heed to the task in hand but will gaze vacantly into space. But not all movements of **Objective Function** are well-practised routines: we can pick up a book from the table, draw the curtains or write a quick message without it involving the senses at all. However, if the book were to be particularly valuable or beautiful, we would pick it up with particular care; if we were to take a sudden hatred to the pattern on the curtains, we would be happy to tear them down as we pull them; if the memo we are writing is more of a vitriolic message or even a coded love-note, then emotion is clearly involved and the function will no longer be objective.

## Movement Sensation

**Movement Sensation,** in Laban terms, is the opposite of **Objective Function**. It may be a movement that gives pleasure or, for that matter, pain, but we are aware of it and so our thoughts would certainly not be elsewhere. The pleasure or pain might be caused by the movement itself, such as running one's hands over pleasing surfaces or picking something up that is too hot to handle – a blind man reading braille with his fingers is certainly using **Movement Sensation** – or the sensation might be caused by emotions not connected with the movement, such as grief or hilarity, but the movement will certainly be affected. The casual swimmer, doing his daily routine of so many lengths in a state of boredom will soon change his style if he suddenly gets cramp or a shark appears!

**Objective Function** and **Movement Sensation** are equally vital where certain skills are concerned. A child learning to write is an obvious example. At first, holding the pencil and trying to copy the letters is very difficult; the movements are laboured and awkward – quite often the tongue comes out to aid concentration – and every movement is a sensation. Gradually, with practice, it gets easier, then, after a couple of years of 'printing', comes the day to learn 'joined-up' writing. This is the preliminary introduction of Flow, the aim being to write words in one continuous, flowing line. After painstakingly following the rules of penmanship with Bound-Flow, Free-Flow gradually takes over, and the writing hardly has to be thought about. Handwriting is a remarkably good example of movement characteristics on a small scale and reveals much of the character of the writer. Some adults, you may have noticed, never get past the printing stage, or they have become stuck in the early, awkward stages of penmanship: they may be brilliant in other ways but their progress in writing came to a stop and Free-Flow was never reached.

Similar to the rigours of learning to write, is the process of learning a musical instrument, say, the piano, or learning a foreign language. At first, both are fraught with difficulties: learning the notes and how to use the fingers, or assimilating the strange pronunciation and grammar will induce a state of Bound-Flow and **Movement Sensation** – every note or every word has to be laboriously thought out and calculated. Then, after much diligence, comes the wonderful moment when the scales run like clockwork and the foreign language becomes fluent and requires little thought – a state of **Objective Function** and Free-Flow has been reached. That is what technique is about. However, the pianist may be able to rattle off difficult passages but playing the piano is not the same as typing; music expresses emotion; it can be uplifting, it can be exciting, it can be passionate; it can be sad or cheerful, in which case the pianist will be very conscious of *how* he plays the notes in order to invest them with feeling. It could be said that pure technique requires **Objective Function** which governs the *what, when* and *where*, while the demands of emotion require **Movement Sensation** which is the *how*.

Looking at the Dynamosphere from the emotional point of view (Figure 52, opposite page), the eight basic efforts now require new terminology. They are no longer purely functional but are affected by feelings, the result of a change in the mover's inner attitude. The Space, Time and Weight continuums remain in place, but their extremes require more suitable names to accommodate the emotion arising from a change in attitude. Flow is no longer neutral but is now very important.

The Weight continuum is now from Light-hearted at the top, meaning buoyant, to Heavy, at the bottom, meaning gloomy; the Space continuum is now from Narrow, meaning pinched, to Pliant, meaning

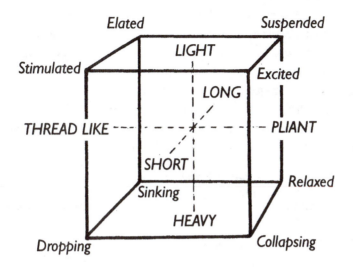

Figure 52:

The Dynamosphere showing the Eight Basic Sensation Efforts, Right side leading

expansive; the Time continuum is now from Short, meaning immediate or urgent, to Long, meaning endless, or easygoing as if 'there's no tomorrow'; the Flow continuum is now from Flowing, meaning uninhibited, to Pausing, meaning inhibited.

Flow is present in all movement activity. Whether it be free or bound, it tends to be a neutral constituent when basic efforts are present and **Objective Function** is dominant. It is a means of communication, not only running outwards to the periphery of our kinesphere but also inwards towards our centre. It enables us to establish a relationship with the world outside. When our emotions are aroused and movement sensation prevails, Flow assumes great importance and can also affect our breathing. Laban talked of fluency, comparing such movement to a fluid substance. The sensation of 'flowing on' can also diminish to 'pausing'. Even in 'pausing', there is the feeling of 'withheld' continuation. Whilst there is life, Flow will never come to a halt.

Now that the ceiling of the cube has changed in terminology from Light to Light-hearted, the four high basic efforts corners require renaming to accommodate the presence of feelings or emotion. Thus, the Floating corner becomes **Suspended,** the Gliding corner becomes **Elated,** the Dabbing corner becomes **Stimulated** and the Flicking corner becomes **Excited.** All these qualities resist the pull of gravity. The base of the cube has now changed from **Strong** to **Heavy** or **Gloomy** and each of the lower require renaming accordingly: the Wringing corner becomes **Relaxing,** the Pressing corner becomes **Sinking,** the Thrusting corner becomes **Dropping** and the Slashing corner becomes **Collapsing.** These four qualities all yield to the pull of gravity.

## Basic Effort Actions

| **Movement Sensation** | **Objective Function** |
|---|---|
| Suspended | Floating |
| *Light/Long/Pliant* | *Light/Sustained/Flexible* |
| Dropping | Thrusting |
| *Heavy/Short/Threadlike* | *Strong/Sudden/Direct* |
| Elated | Gliding |
| *Light/Long/Threadlike* | *Light/Sustained/Direct* |
| Collapsing | Slashing |
| *Heavy/Short/Pliant* | *Strong/Sudden/Flexible* |
| Stimulated | Dabbing |
| *Light/Short/Threadlike* | *Light/Sudden/Direct* |
| Relaxed | Wringing |
| *Heavy/Long/Pliant* | *Strong/Sustained/Flexible* |
| Excited | Flicking |
| *Light/Short/Pliant* | *Light/Sudden/Flexible* |
| Sinking | Pressing |
| *Heavy/Long/Threadlike* | *Strong/Sustained/Direct* |

## The Effect of Movement on the Breath

It is clear that we breathe in and out from the day we are born to the day we die but there are a surprising number of ways of achieving this process – from sniffs to gasps and from sneezes to coughs. When we are inactive our breathing is reasonably even, particularly when we are asleep. However, most of our activities affect the way we breathe. Take a simple gesture like lifting and opening your arms wide – automatically you will breathe in. To breathe *out* on such a gesture would be difficult and would feel wrong. You only have to try both to be convinced. Dropping your arms will cause you to breathe out and even more so if you collapse your body down with them. It is generally true to say that light, upward movements cause you to breathe in while heavy, downward movements cause you to breathe out. This coincides rather well with Laban's Gathering and Scattering: as you stoop down to gather you will breathe out and as you lift to scatter you will breathe in.

Any gesture that consists of a strong slash or a thrust requires an intake of breath first which is exhaled with the gesture. A tennis serve is a good example and one you can easily simulate; as you lift and toss the ball aloft, you will breathe in; then, as you take a swipe at the ball you will expel nearly all your breath. It goes with the movement. A more constant energetic activity, such as running, demands much more breath than usual, and the more vigorous the activity, the quicker the breaths need to be. This is all to do with the using up of oxygen in the muscles which needs to be replaced, thus causing a constant dialogue between the brain and the diaphragm.

Some activities, such as lifting or pushing a heavy object (the grand piano again!) require that we take a deep breath and lock it. In other words, we are holding a full breath inside ourselves, making us feel bigger and stronger and giving us added momentum.

It is important that we allow the rhythm of our breathing to respond to the prevailing rhythm of our movements. Not to do so, and this does happen, can cause lack of co-ordination and dysfunction. In music, phrasing is all to do with breath: so it should be in movement. Dancers, in particular, should watch this; breathing the phrases is far more pleasing than counting the beats, and there is far less likelihood of getting out of breath. For singers and speakers, where the outgoing breath serves a distinct purpose, the intake of breath tends to be quicker, while the outgoing breath is of necessity slower – sometimes considerably so.

## The Effect of Emotions on the Breath

Just as physical movement can interfere with any regular rhythm in breathing, so can the emotions, and for the same reason: that more oxygen is needed to cope with the situation. An obvious example is the impact on the emotions of surprise, unpleasant or pleasant. Unpleasant surprise, in the form of being given a fright, will cause a sharp intake of breath. For instance, if you were suddenly threatened by a mugger, after the sharp intake of breath you would probably hold it in a freeze while you wonder what to do, having taken in the maximum amount of oxygen. On the other hand, if the cause of the fright turns out to be a friend, as soon as you realise this you would exhale the breath with sheer relief. By contrast, the breath of pleasant surprise is just that – a surprise and pleasant. For instance, imagine unexpectedly bumping into an old friend you haven't seen for a long time; you are delighted – your face lights up, your mouth opens and you take a deep breath of pleasure. If, on the other hand you were to breathe in only through your nose, your friend could easily get the impression that you were not pleased to see him at all!

Two extreme examples of emotions strongly affecting the breath are laughing and crying, both remarkably similar due to the convulsions of the diaphragm. Laughing could be said to be freer than crying, especially on the intake of breath; when exhaling, the breath is spasmodically blocked, causing the sound of laughter. The intake of breath when giving in to grief is frequently blocked by closed vocal cords, thereby making a vocal sound on ingressive air; when exhaling, the breath is still spasmodically blocked, resulting in short bursts of anguished sound.

Another very common example of the emotions affecting the breath is the sigh. Although this can be caused purely by physical inertia, more often it is the result of an unconscious pause in breathing. We all tend to do it when our mind is preoccupied, either with something pleasant or with some nagging problem – we forget to breathe in. Eventually, the brain realises this and sends an urgent message down to the diaphragm, 'Look here, I need oxygen!' And immediately we take in a very deep breath and release it rather noisily so that it is usually plainly evident to those nearby. People notice sighs. They think, 'Is he worried about something, or is he in love?' With lovers, the sigh is almost a hallmark of their state of mind, as they mope for their absent loved ones, but it is less a sign of romance than the brain's call for oxygen.

These examples remind us that the solar plexus, that central complex of nerves and blood vessels, situated at the pit of the stomach, is the seat of the emotions. It is here that we feel the heaviness of grief, and it is from here that we feel the upsurge of joy. To put it in plain terms, our feelings and emotions emanate from our guts and when we breathe deeply, it is to there that we reach. That is why in creative work, it is so often referred to as our 'centre'.

Of course, physical states, apart from respiratory ailments, can also affect our breath: a sudden, sharp pain will cause a sudden, sharp intake of breath (similar to the breath of unpleasant surprise), but the most obvious manifestation is yawning. We all know that yawning denotes tiredness, but there is more to it than that: the tiredness causes the breathing activity to become slack and inefficient, causing a lack of oxygen. Here, again, the brain sends an SOS down to the diaphragm so that the whole respiratory tract opens up (including the mouth) in order quickly to get as much air in as possible. Truly, the human body is a miraculous machine.

# 5

## *The Movement in Sound and Voice*

All sound is created by some sort of movement. Without movement there would be silence.

Sound and light have much in common in that they both travel in waves which have crests and troughs and are similar to the ripples in water which move outward from the point where, for instance, a stone has been dropped in. However, both sound and light can be channelled in one direction by fencing it in, as in the case of a megaphone or spotlight.

Laban made us aware that when we move we disturb space. It would be equally true to say that when we speak, sing or shout, we disturb space, or in this case the air, by creating vibrations which travel through the air in the form of sound waves. As the wave passes, the air molecules crowd together then separate, which produces a pulse or vibrato. The actual sensation of hearing the sound occurs when the waves reach our ears. So, however quiet we try to be, creeping about so as not to disturb someone, we are making vibrations which can be heard by sensitive ears, such as those of a dog or a cat or a blind person.

In this book, we have paid a great deal of attention to arms and legs, hands and feet, the torso and the head, but we have not considered the areas that produce the voice. A well-tuned body is more likely to produce a well-tuned voice, but that is not always the case. The human voice is part of a wonderful machine that is very much taken for granted. As children, we learn to speak by copying those around us, and we tend to leave it at that. It is worthy of note that a baby, gurgling away in its pram, will go through nearly every phonetic segment of all the languages in the world – a state of perfect potential; only when it hears the voices of those around – mother, father and Auntie Flo – will that baby start to select the sounds it hears from the vast array available to it and reduce them to the few that are necessary to make itself understood. So let us examine this wonderful machine and see how it works.

## The Vocal Mechanism

The vocal mechanism is like a highly complex musical instrument in which there are many interlinking components. Put into simple terms, and continuing the musical analogy, these components can be divided into four sections: the **Bellows,** the **Reed,** the **Articulators** and the **Resonators.**

The **Bellows,** needless to say, are concerned with blowing air through the instrument in much the same way as the bellows of an old pipe-organ. Without air, no vocal sound can be made. Included in this section are the lungs, the diaphragm, the abdominal muscles, the ribs, and the muscles between the ribs (intercostals), and windpipe. At the top of the windpipe is the **Reed,** which is the larynx or voice-box which produces the notes. Without this vital piece of equipment no vocal sound can be made either. The rest of the musical instrument is concerned with enhancing the sound that the **Bellows** and the **Reed** have made. The **Articulators,** mostly contained in the mouth, formulate this sound into something more specific, such as words, while the **Resonators,** which are mostly in the nasal area, amplify it and project it towards the **Receiver** – in other words, somebody's ear.

Here is a list of the main components of the vocal mechanism, beginning at its lowest point, which corresponds more or less to the order of use when producing a sound.

> The diaphragm
>
> The abdominal muscles
>
> The ribs and intercostal muscles
>
> The lungs
>
> The windpipe
>
> The larynx or voice-box
>
> The throat or pharynx

The jaw

The tongue

The soft palate

The hard palate

The teeth

The lips

The nasal cavity

The nose

The maxillary sinuses

The nasal sinuses

The frontal sinuses

The top of the skull

Nearly all these components have a more fundamental use than producing a voice.

The **diaphragm** is a dome-shaped muscular partition which separates the thoracic and abdominal cavities; it is attached all round to the bottom of the rib-cage, rather like a trampoline, and its main function is its domination of the mechanics of breathing.

The primary function of the **ribs** is to protect the heart and other vital organs. Between them are the web-like intercostal muscles which expand and contract with breathing.

The primary function of the **lungs** is to supply the blood with oxygen, without which we could not live, and to expel carbon dioxide, which is the air we vibrate when we speak or sing.

The **larynx** is a triangular-shaped structure of cartilage and muscle situated at the top of the **windpipe.** It is surmounted by a leaf-shaped lid, called the epiglottis, which closes like a trap-door when we swallow. Thus, one of its primary functions is to prevent food or liquid from entering the windpipe and filling the lungs. This miraculous little box contains the **vocal cords,** which are a pair of tough but extremely flexible bands of muscle. When brought together edge to edge, they can convert the upward flow of air into sound vibrations and by stretching or loosening can produce different pitches.

The **pharynx** is the space immediately above the larynx which we are very aware of when we have a sore throat. Primarily, the pharynx is a common passageway for air going to and from the lungs and for the swallowing of food. It is also an echo-chamber and is the first enhancer of the fundamental tone emitted by the vocal cords.

The **mouth** is primarily used for eating, of course, but it consists of several areas that are vital to vocal production. Most important is the **tongue**, the primary function of which is to give the sensation of taste and to push food around the mouth so that it gets properly chewed in readiness for swallowing. As an organ of speech, it has the greatest responsibility in transforming pure vocal tone into actual words. Not for nothing is the word 'tongue' synonymous with language. Its complex muscular structure makes it a virtuoso in the mouth. In fact, the tongue is a dancer! The primary function of the **jaw**, armed as it is with teeth, is to bite and chew food. Vocally, the jaw forms the base of the articulation mechanism; a notorious repository of tension, it is important that it should remain free.

The **soft palate** and the **hard palate**, together with the **alveolar ridge**, the bony prominence behind the top front teeth, form the roof of the mouth, without which few words, as we know them, could be pronounced properly, if at all, for it is against them and the **teeth** that the tongue wields its remarkable dexterity in the formation of words. The **soft palate** is more mobile than we think and needs to be in the right place.

The **lips** are the front door of the mouth and form a pleasant pink edge to the obicularis oris muscle that surrounds the front of the mouth. The mucus membrane commences just inside the lips and continues to line the whole of the respiratory and digestive systems. Having countless nerve endings just below the surface, lips are extremely sensitive and are pleasure seekers – they like sipping and kissing; they can smile or tremble with emotion. Vocally, they contribute enormously to the formation of words.

The **nasal cavity** is also lined with mucus membrane and its primary function as part of the airway is to warm and moisten air as it is inhaled. Within it are the protective reflexes of sneezing and the olfactory receptors that provide the sense of smell. It serves the voice as a major resonator, being like the body of a violin.

The primary function of the **nose** is to provide two air vents through which we inhale and exhale. It is like the prow of a ship and points the voice in the right direction. Backed up by the facial resonators, it is the last outpost of the voice before it travels across space.

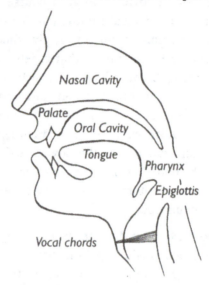

Figure 53: The Upper Vocal Mechanism

The **facial sinuses** are perhaps the only part of the vocal system that don't have a primary function apart from acting as echo chambers for the voice. As such, they are small rounded cavities in the skull which have an amazing capacity for amplifying the voice far beyond its fundamental level. We have four pairs of sinuses: the **maxillary** sinuses either side of the nose, below the eyes and above the top teeth; the two pairs of nasal sinuses, the **sphenoidal** sinuses on either side of the nose bone and the **ethmoidal** sinuses, adjacent behind the bridge of the nose, making the whole area potentially very vibrant and resonant, and the **frontal** sinuses, so-called because they are situated in the frontal bone of the skull just above each eyebrow.

The primary function of the **skull**, of course, is to provide a strong protective case for the brain, but this, depending on the looseness and freedom of the muscles governing the head, is also a remarkable resonator as you can easily tell if you place your hand gently on top of someone's head while they are speaking.

The **spine** is also a great contributor to the vocal mechanism because, unless we are lying down, it is responsible for holding everything in place and, as a resonator, it provides a good sounding board.

All the components of the vocal mechanism should work in perfect conjuction with each other; if the sound is poor, it means that one or more of the components is not in the right place at the right time, or is being misused, or is not being used at all. Some of these components don't actually move, but they certainly vibrate; these, in particular, are the pharynx, the hard palate, the nasal cavity, the sinuses and the skull.

Producing the voice needs tension – but in the right muscles. When a voice is badly produced it is because the wrong muscles are tense or there is not enough tension in the right muscles. The acquisition of any skill depends on the right muscles being used in the right order and at the right time. For the vocal mechanism to function efficiently, it is necessary for the whole body to be in a harmonious state, which is where Laban's work is so valuable. He can help us to release ourselves from the shackles of modern, civilised living. Awkwardness and lack of coordination should disappear, along with certain negative responses that affect our physical efficiency, such as shyness and the reluctance to make fools of ourselves.

Bodily movement can be very helpful in freeing the voice from unnecessary tensions, after which the body needs to be comparatively still in order to let the voice move, just as the violin needs to stay reasonably still and leave the movement to the bow. For instance, if you jump about while you are speaking or singing, your voice will be punctuated with jerky pulses. However, in its 'stillness', the body must in no way be fixed; it is a breathing, flexible stillness where certain muscles need to be used and others not.

Producing the voice requires energy, and energy depends on effort – not effort that is straining at the leash or bursting blood vessels, but the right amount of effort to create the necessary amount of energy for the task in hand. Laban has shown us very clearly that effort is not just strong and forceful but is equally an effort when it is light and minimal. Reaching any standard in a skill requires some sort of effort; ideally, the effort used should be no more and no less than that which is required. Using the analogy of the violin again, the violinist who presses too heavily on the strings with his bow will produce an unpleasant scraping sound whereas an insufficient and diffident pressure will produce a hazy, hesitant sound. It is almost exactly the same situation with the voice; pressing the air too hard against the vocal cords will produce a rough, hoarse voice whereas feeble use of the breath will produce a wispy, breathy voice.

The first movement that should occur in the vocal mechanism to produce a vocal sound is the diaphragm pulling down towards the pelvis causing air to be drawn into the lungs. The abdominal muscles should then come into action and firm themselves round the diaphragm to give it a firm base. From this firm base, the diaphragm rebounds upwards, pushing the air out of the lungs to form a column of air in the windpipe. To transform this column of air into voice, it has to be interfered with by certain obstacles, the first of which will be the vocal cords. These may close firmly like double doors before the breath reaches them, causing the air to force its way through the closed edges so that the sound commences with a glottal stop which gives the effect of a kick or small cough at the beginning of the sound. You can get the feeling of this by doing a similar action with your lips. Take a good breath then close your lips and release the breath through them on a vigorous 'p' sound. Compare this with an 'ugh' bursting through your larynx.

A more pleasant way of vibrating the air column is to let it pass through the larynx *before* closing the vocal cords on it. This occurs when you say or sing a word like 'heart'. The 'h' is a soft noise of friction as the breath passes through the half-closed vocal cords. This is the 'whisper position' and can be compared to the 'f' sound through half-closed lips.

Lips can also provide a good example of how the vocal cords vibrate: take a good breath and breathe out vigorously through closed lips on a 'brrrr' sound, as we do when we're feeling cold. Here, the lips flap noisily together and apart at about ten times per second, which is similar to what the vocal cords do, but they do it considerably faster, from about seventy times per second to more than two thousand times per second, depending on the pitch.

Once the voice is vibrating through the larynx, the breath in the pharynx above it vibrates in sympathy, thus increasing the volume of the sound. This is the beginning of the resonance process.

As the sound rises, the next source of interference is the soft palate, that soft membrane at the back of the roof of the mouth. This can be raised or lowered, either blocking off the mouth or the nose. When the mouth is blocked off, the voice goes into the nasal cavity and acquires an unpleasant nasal whine; when the nose is blocked off, the voice sounds 'adenoidal', as though the speaker has a bad cold. Ideally, the soft palate should be in a midway position so that the voice can enter the mouth to be articulated *and* enter the nasal cavity for further resonance. From the roof of the mouth (hard palate) and from the nasal cavity, the voice reaches its final resonance chambers, the sinuses and skull, ready to cause a disturbance in space.

To produce good tone, the outgoing breath should be concentrated into a column of intensity, rather than for it to limp along and leak through the vocal cords. Here are some good ways to mobilise the breath:

- 1. After a good deep inhalation, which you should feel all round your waist, blow out a candle or lighted match. As you breathe in and focus your attention on the flame, you will automatically round your lips. In order to create the necessary force in the outgoing breath, the diaphragm will pull inwards and upwards. Blowing out a candle usually elicits a short sharp breath though it can be done equally well with a long, strong, even breath. Try both, and always check that your diaphragm pulls in when you blow rather than pushing your stomach out.

- 2. Try blowing the flame out down your nose. This requires particular focus because the airstream is more vertical. In fact, you have to find your target. Your lips should be closed, of course, forcing the breath to come down the narrow outlet of your nostrils, causing a strong draught. The advantage of this exercise is that it makes you very aware of what you are doing with your breath and where it is going.

- 3. Returning to your mouth, take a good, deep breath and send it out on a very strong 'SHH' sound, as though you are annoyed with a noisy child. Here again, the contraction of the diaphragm, inwards and upwards, should be apparent.

- 4. Repeat the last exercise, only this time separate your upper and lower teeth with the width of two fingers (don't put them far in and try not to bite them). At first, the 'SHH' may sound lost in the void and quite unlike the sound you made before, in which case you must re-arrange your tongue until it sounds identical to the previous exercise. Make the 'SHH' as long and as vigorous as you can.

- 5. The next stage is to involve the vocal cords in the flow of the 'SHH' by adding the vowel of 'EE', making a bold 'SHHEE'. Be sure the 'SHH' is really strong and at least two seconds long before voicing the vowel. Do not in any way involve your throat or neck muscles. Try this several times in the easy, middle area of your speech pitch.

- 6. This time, elongate the vowel onto actual note pitches so that your voice graduates from speech to singing. If you have a piano or keyboard, this is ideal but, if not, think of a note clearly before singing it.

All this shows how using the vocal mechanism is a series of movements which rely on the passage of breath to produce a vocal sound. As for making that sound into words, that is where the dancing tongue comes in, which needs to interfere with that breath and vocal tone to produce the sounds that form words. These sounds are known as vowels and consonants.

**Forming Words: Vowels and Consonants**

What is the difference, you might say? The simplest view is that vowels are 'tone' and that consonants are 'noise' but the official phonetic distinction between them is that of stricture, which refers to a temporary narrowing or closure of the speech tract, causing audible friction, which is characteristic of nearly all consonants. An obvious example of this is 'SHH', where the lips are constricted, the teeth are fairly close together and the tongue is curled down behind them, making a three-fold blockage. Some consonants involve the voice, such as L, M, N and V. Others, such as F, P, T and S are pure strictured breath. You have only to compare them to see that they are all different ways of interfering with the flow of air.

Vowels, on the other hand, are not formed by stricture but by making different shapes of the mouth, which are determined by the tongue, lips and soft palate. Thus, the acoustic energy is banded into powerful forms which give each vowel its identity. The prime mover is the tongue, which flicks between consonants and vowels and glides through diphthongs and triphthongs with utmost dexterity. And how does it know how to do this? By its owner hearing other tongues speaking and, by instinct and empathy, copying them. This is only partially successful, for it has to be said, some tongues only give an approximation of the words they are supposed to be saying; they wallow about in the mouth in much the same manner as some people wallow about when trying to dance. What is needed is some choreography for this wayward dancer that will pin-point the positions as accurately as possible. But how can one pinpoint the often fleeting position of a vowel as it changes to another vowel or consonant? The answer came from the world of phonetics where a chart was devised which has much in common with Laban's ideas in using the crystals as guides for movement. This chart, however, is two-dimensional and represents a side view of the mouth.

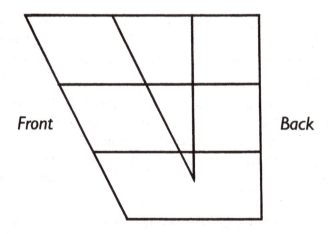

Figure 54: The phonetic chart of the mouth

Vowels are measured by the closeness or distance of the front, middle or back of the tongue from the roof of the mouth. The two most identifiable vowels were found to be 'EE', where the front of the tongue is raised close to the hard palate, and 'AH', where the back of the tongue is lowered far down from the palate. Using these two vowels as hinges or pivots, another six clearly definable vowels were mapped out. These are known as the eight cardinal vowels, four at the front of the mouth, measured in equal degrees downwards from 'EE', and four at the back of the mouth, measured in equal degrees upwards from 'AH', looking like this on the chart:

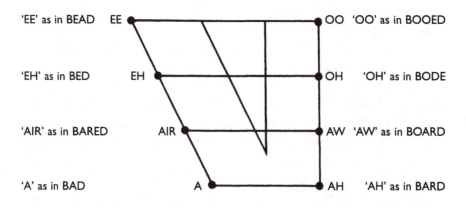

Figure 55: Chart of the eight Cardinal Vowels

If you say each of these eight cardinal vowels in rotation, starting with EE and ending with OO, you should feel a distinct forward-moving circular progress in your mouth which is akin to the movement of the Wheel Plane.

It is worth noting that, owing to the inadequacy of the alphabet – only five letters, A, E, I, O and U to represent more than twenty vowel sounds – it is necessary to use words to identify the sound of the vowels. However, there is a phonetic alphabet which can depict almost any sound, which is comparable in its way to Labanotation, which can depict almost every movement.

Apart from the eight Cardinal Vowels, there are many other vowel sounds, which are known as variants. An important vowel that is not a cardinal is the central sound of 'ER' (or 'eu' as it would be in French), which is frequently uttered when a person is undecided as to what to say or do and the tongue is in a neutral position.

Figure 56: The tongue in the neutral position of 'eu' or 'er'

A word should be said about diphthongs and triphthongs, as we use them all the time. Diphthongs are two vowels joined in a slide, as in the word 'day', which is 'DEH' sliding to 'EE', or 'how', which is 'HAH' sliding to 'OO'. A triphthong consists of three vowels joined by slides, as in 'hour', which is 'AH' sliding to 'OO' sliding to 'ER'. From this you can see how the tongue has certain pathways to follow in order to produce words. Sometimes, the pathway is quite complicated as in a word like 'actually'. Here the tongue starts with the vowel of 'A', before coping with the contrasting consonants of 'c' and 't'; the 't' leads nicely into 'EE' before quickly sliding across the top of the mouth to 'OO'; 'OO' slides quickly to 'UH' (a variant of 'AH'), which is followed by the voiced consonant of a double 'l' before finishing with 'EE' again. Phew! Quite often, the tongue moves through areas of unwanted sound as in the word 'yard', which is 'EE' sliding imperceptibly through 'ER' all the way to 'AHD'. These fleeting moments between vowels are similar to those fleeting moments between one incomplete effort and another.

The jaw is a notorious repository of tension, and much energy is wasted because of it. In repose, the jaw should be dropped, leaving quite a space between the top and bottom teeth. If the teeth are touching, a certain amount of tension will be holding the jaw up. Try this for yourself: seal your lips lightly and consciously relax your jaw so that it drops. Your lips don't need to part and you should be able to waggle your jaw from side to side without your teeth scraping each other. You can also try talking while doing this sideways movement. Apart from this, the jaw shouldn't be exercised as it gets quite enough already, but letting go of it is important. For the tongue to have maximum efficiency, it is necessary to ensure that it is independent from the jaw.

### Exercises to separate the tongue from the jaw

- 1. Breathe in, opening your mouth so there is at least half an inch between your upper and lower teeth and say: GA-GA-GA-GA-GA-GA-GA. The back and middle of your tongue should rise and fall vigorously but this will not happen if you move your jaw so check in the mirror that your jaw remains loose but still. If necessary, place a fingertip between your upper and lower incisors so that your jaw can't move.

- 2. Repeat the preparation in the previous exercise and say: KA-KA-KA-KA-KA-KA-KA. The movement of your tongue should be similar to GA, except that you will be aware of the outward flow of breath.

- 3. Without using any voice but at most whispering, breathe in doing the GA-GAs and breathe out on the KA-KAs. This is most beneficial.

- 4. Alternate two vowels: EE-AH-EE-AH-EE-AH-EE-AH. Here the tip of your tongue should remain in place behind your bottom front teeth, while the middle of your tongue goes forwards (EE) and backwards (AH) like a shuttle.

### Speaking and Singing

Considering that the same mechanism is used for both speaking and singing, it is an interesting phenomenon that most people are not overly self-conscious when it comes to speaking but the reverse is the case when it comes to singing. When asked why this should be, the usual reply is the worry of pitching notes or staying in tune. Coupled with this is the matter of keeping some sort of time. This is particularly true if a recognizable tune is to be the result. But there is more to it than that. To begin with, everyday speaking is something we tend to take for granted and barely give a thought to it. Thus it is very much an **Objective Function** especially when no emotion is involved. Singing, on the other hand, is nearly always the direct result of an emotional response and is more akin to **Movement Sensation**. Also, singing is much more *revealing* than speaking, with the result that most people don't want to reveal themselves to that extent! But the major difference is that people don't listen to themselves talking but they do listen to themselves singing and are put off! The answer is *don't.* As with dancing or any physical movement, the drive should come from within and be a release of energy – without negative thoughts. It would be ridiculous if every time you raised your arm in a gesture you thought to yourself, 'I look a fool doing this,' which is the equivalent of what so many people do when prevailed upon to sing: they think they sound awful with the result that they probably do. Everybody has the right to sound at least pleasant when they sing.

Good vocal tone requires mental free-flow (see section on Flow on pages 127–8) combined with a certain physical bound-flow in the control of the voice. A voice running away out of control is like a bicycle without breaks. Laughter has a lovely feeling of freedom but there is a distinct locking of the breath that produces a series of broken sounds; there is a great deal of difference in saying 'Ha! Ha! Ha!' as written in books and playscripts, and actually laughing. In speaking, when 'throwing' the voice with as much abandon as possible, there should be a wonderful feeling of release, as when cheering or shouting 'Hooray!' The feeling should be far removed from any restriction or constriction.

All notes, whether sung or played on a musical instrument, consist of a fundamental vibration, accompanied by overtones or reverberations. The more free the voice or instrument is to vibrate, the richer will be the overtones. If you tap a finely shaped glass or bowl it will ring beautifully, but if you hold the glass or bowl with your other hand, you will 'damp' the sound and the fundamental ring will be deadened as well as any overtones. In the same way, our voices will produce a far better sound if our bodies are free of unnecessary tensions and the cavities in the skull are free to enhance the vibrations – which brings us to the subject of humming.

## Resonance: The Benefit of Humming

Most of us know what it is to hum a tune, or just hum something, without giving it a thought; it is a way of singing without having one's mouth open, making it almost a private activity. There are those who will hum quite absent-mindedly as they involve themselves in some task, whereas they would be very reluctant to open their mouths and sing. Emotionally speaking, humming is a release of tension; it is a pleasant sensation and soothes the feelings. However, when some thought is given to it and it is efficiently done with **Movement Sensation**, it is one of the most effective ways of improving the resonance in the voice. With the lips closed, the initial vibration of the vocal cords (the fundamental) can resound through all the cavities of the skull and thus increase in amplitude.

We all know that in order to hum, the lips should be sealed – what the French call *bouche fermée*. However, the *bouche* should not be so *fermée* as to be clamped shut. While the lips are sealed, the lower jaw should be loosely dropped as far as comfort will allow, thus making a large vibrating chamber of the mouth. Humming may seem to be predominantly concerned with the nose but, without the involvement of the mouth, a great deal of sound is lost. It is therefore important that, when humming, the back of the tongue doesn't rise and block the mouth off. The diagram shows how the vibrations from the unblocked mouth reach the facial sinuses through the hard palate.

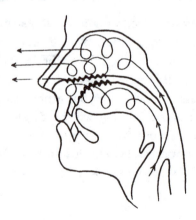

Figure 57: Humming vibrations

### To initiate a good humming sound:

- Take a breath and say in a good rounded voice the word 'HUM'.

- Now lightly seal your lips and, as you breathe in, lower your jaw to a comfortable extremity.

- Keeping your lips sealed, repeat the word 'HUM', letting the 'H' aspirate itself down your nose, followed by the humming sound.

- Repeat the process at different pitches, always making sure that you aspirate the 'H' down your nose. Follow this with actual note pitches.

- From humming it is very pleasant to release the sound on to an open 'AH', resulting in 'HUM-AH'. Let your lips part with the feeling of a smile but not a rictus-like grin. You can try this with various gestures, matching the physical release with the release of 'AH'. It is also most beneficial to walk about while vocalising which helps to avoid tension in unwanted places.

There are certain movements which are helpful in improving tone in the voice, but care should be taken that at no time should the neck muscles supporting the head be tense, otherwise the resonance capacity of the head is severely impaired. The head should sit lightly on top of the spine. The old image of a ping-pong ball borne aloft on top of a fountain still holds good. A good way to achieve this is to roll down your spine.

- Rock your head slowly forwards and backwards several times, feeling the weight of it each time it drops. Then drop it forward and let the weight of your head seem to pull down your spine like a drooping plant. As you curl down your spine, let your shoulders and arms hang loose. Keep your balance by letting your knees bend a little.

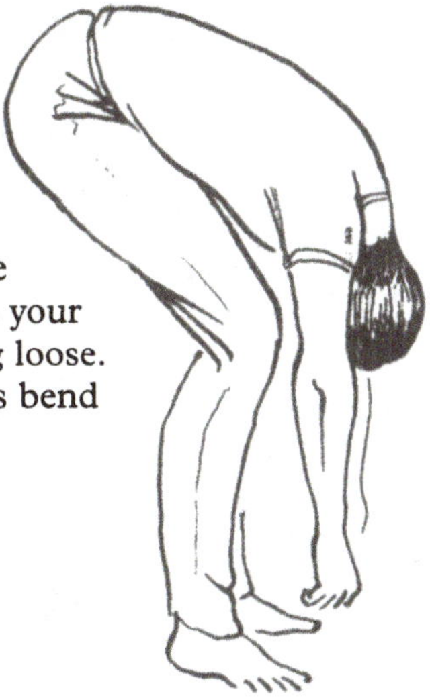

Figure 58: The 'Drooping Plant'

● As you hang down from your waist, gently shake your head, shoulders and arms. Pause long enough to feel how heavy your head is, hanging like a coconut or heavy fruit on a stem, then slowly uncurl your spine, letting your shoulders and arms fall into place, your neck and head coming up last. Your head should feel light enough to blow away! The ability to let your head hang loose or to float it lightly on top of your spinal column greatly increases its resonating capacity.

Apart from walking or doing a gentle trot, other helpful movements, particularly when singing, are making wide, floating gestures with your arms. When singing scales or arpeggios, hold on to a chair or something firm and, as the voice rises, do a slow knees-bend or plié. This helps to involve your hips and pelvis as part of the sounding board. As you go down, your voice will soar!

# 6

## *Incomplete Efforts*

Incomplete effort actions do not mean half-finished tasks. They occur when one of the three continuums (Space, Time or Weight) is barely stressed, and its input is almost entirely absent. Sometimes the presence of Flow is discernible, but in a situation where extreme caution and precision is needed, it would be unwise to attempt to use Free-Flow. For example, an apprentice learning to use dangerous machinery would need to exercise extreme caution; an over-confident approach could lead to serious injury. Bound-Flow would be a more suitable option. On the other hand, the highly skilled workman or a self-confident and outgoing person would be more likely to use Free-Flow as natural expressive movement qualities.

So far, we have discussed people who have clearly defined attitudes of either caution or confidence. However, someone with an extremely casual attitude is neither sudden nor sustained in his actions. Instead he will move without any definite concern for Time whilst maintaining the expressive qualities of Space and Weight.

Incomplete effort actions can be seen as transitions between one basic effort action and the next. Basic actions can momentarily give way to more expressive behaviour before returning, once again, to the original routine actions. A typist may stop her work to pat her new hair-do with satisfaction; this will break the monotony for a moment before she returns to her work.

Another variant is where two basic effort actions seem to merge in one of the three continuums. For example, a man delivering heavy sacks of potatoes off the back of his lorry will use a strong, sudden and flexible effort to hoist a sack onto his back. Once there, he will change his action from sudden to something more sustained. His basic actions will have been from **Slashing** (sudden) to **Wringing** (sustained). Certainly no casual approach here. His attitude towards Time may be indefinite but Space and Weight maintain their qualities of strength and flexibility. The resulting movement quality lies somewhere between the two basic actions of **Slashing** and **Wringing**, that is, **Slash-wring**.

A traveller in London's underground in the rush hour may join the crowd trying to get onto the train before the doors close. Joining the **Pressing** crowd and not wishing to get caught in the doors, he gives a final thrust to get inside, changing the Time factor from sustained to sudden. His actions have been **Pressing** and **Thrusting**. His attitude towards Space, for the moment, is 'on hold' whilst **Press** and **Thrust** maintain their attitudes of strength and sudden or sustained Time. The resulting quality lies somewhere between the basic actions of **Pressing** and **Thrusting**, that is **Press-thrust**.

*Other examples of incomplete efforts are:*

**Flick-float** occurs in small movements of the hands and fingers such as tossing or throwing away small, light objects, removing fluff from clothing or twiddling one's fingers.

**Dab-glide** occurs as a transitional effort when Dabbing develops into Gliding as in the act of dabbing on makeup and then smoothing it over your face.

**Thrust-press** occurs when Thrusting develops into Pressing and often occurs when manual tasks are carried out, such as dealing with an obstinate drawer: first you thrust the drawer in but it stops half-way so you change your thrust to a push or Press.

**Slash-flick** occurs when Slashing develops into Flicking as when making a strong movement in the direction of a fly followed by flicking it away.

The incomplete efforts not only appear as links between adjacent basic efforts, but they are also fundamental to human behaviour. Speech, for instance, is often accompanied by small movements which are incomplete efforts. Try to observe yourself doing these actions so that you can learn the feel of each one as well as its name. For the performer, in particular, an understanding of incomplete effort actions is invaluable for showing the inner depths of a character. These inner attitudes heighten our moods, thereby, encouraging more expressive movement behaviour showing that human beings are not automatons but are subject to all sorts of tiny emotional influences. Inner attitudes can be deliberate or subconscious, significant or purely functional.

## Mental Effort Preceding Action:
## Attention, Intention, Decision and Precision

Before carrying out any operational task, our body and mind prepare themselves; the mind will 'concentrate' on the job ahead and our body is 'at the ready'. This preparation becomes visible in very small, muscular body movements. There are four phases: Attention, Intention, Decision and Precision. They may appear simultaneously, in any order, or one or more may be omitted.

**Attention is related to the motion factor of Space.** We can orientate ourselves so that we can focus on whatever attracts our attention, either focusing directly, without distraction, or indirectly in a circuitous, roundabout manner.

**Intention is related to the motion factor of Weight** and usually follows Attention. Intention can be a strong desire to do something or a slight intention.

**Decision is related to the motion factor of Time.** Decisions can be made smoothly, or unexpectedly and suddenly, or 'mulled over' and arrived at over a long or sustained period of Time.

**Precision is related to the motion factor of Flow.** Precison (or progression) involves the final anticipatory moment before accomplishing the actual task. The Flow factor may be controlled and bound or it can be utterly unrestrained and free.

A typical example of the above four phases of mental effort preceding action would be when your **attention** is drawn to a book lying on the table. You then have the **intention** of picking it up. Having made the **decision** to do so, your **precision** determines how you will pick it up.

However, actions do not always follow through to such a smooth conclusion. Your attention may have been directed to the book and you intend to pick it up, but the telephone rings. At once your attention and intention is directed to the telephone and the book is forgotten. Before you can answer it, the phone stops ringing so, slightly peeved, your attention and intention return to the book and you decide to pick it up but, possibly, your precision is impaired and you grab it carelessly and drop it. So, you have to start all over again.

These attitudes are often transitions between one basic effort and another. Laban distinguished these inner attitudes as representing three pairs of opposites:

| Incomplete Effort | | Emphasis on Movement | Giving information about |
|---|---|---|---|
| 1 (a) | | Space and Time | Where and When |
| 1 (b) | | Flow and Weight | How and What |
| 2 (a) | | Space and Flow | Where and How |
| 2 (b) | | Weight and Time | What and When |
| 3 (a) | | Space and Weight | Where and What |
| 3 (b) | | Time and Flow | When and How |

Laban explains that 'It is difficult to attach names to these variations of incomplete efforts as they are concerned with pure movement experience and expression'. He suggests that we should perform the bodily actions with the two motion factors as stated, using one element at a time and then both simultaneously.

**1a)** In this first example in the first pair of opposites, the emphasis is on motion factors Space and Time giving us information about Where and When.

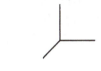

Graph Space and Time Factors

**Space** (as in where) is related to Attention.

**i) Focusing with concentration on an object or person.** As when a young man shows great interest in a pretty girl.

**ii) Regarding in a diffused, flexible manner.** As when you give fellow travellers a fleeting glance, showing only partial or no interest in them.

**Time** (as in when) is related to Decision.

**iii) Sudden.** As when the young man is so attracted to the girl, he promptly asks her out to dinner.

**iv) Gradual.** As when the girl in question needs some time to consider his invitation.

**Space-Time**

**v) Focusing on something with sudden concentration.** As when watching a horse race. From the moment of 'They're off!' all attention is riveted.

**vi) Focusing on something with gradual concentration.** As when glancing idly out of the window, you're not sure whether it's a bird or some animal on the lawn so you watch till it gives you a clue.

**vii) A sudden diffused regard.** As when a dozing traveller suddenly opens his eyes, uncertain where he is.

**viii) A gradual diffused regard.** As when a traveller in a car or train has some distance to go and looks around him in a semi-comatose manner.

The above examples of Space-Time demonstrate an awareness which may be certain or uncertain. Laban suggested the characteristics of the incomplete effort of Space-Time were representative of an **Awake Mode**.

**1b)** In this second example, making up the first pair of opposites, the emphasis is on the motion factors Flow and Weight giving us information about How and What.

Graph Flow and Weight Factors

**Flow** (as in how) is related to Precision.

**i) Bold.** As when wielding a brush with great ease, whilst white-washing a wall.

**ii) Diffused.** As when white-washing a wall with an uneven surface.

**Weight** (as in what) is related to Intention.

**iii) Gloomy.** As when you are searching everywhere and cannot find your glasses.

**iv) Exalted.** As when planning to cook your favourite recipe for appreciative friends.

**Flow – Weight.**

**v) Diffused and Gloomy.** As when you cannot see clearly enough to find your missing glasses.

**vi) Diffused and Exalted.** As when you have found your glasses but have not yet put them on.

**vii) Bold and Gloomy.** As when you are white-washing a wall with great abandon, tired of the boring job but determined to get it finished.

**viii). Bold and Exalted.** The footballer who will take the free kick has to be bold – and, if he scores goal, he will be overjoyed – along with a great many other people!

Without the Space factor there is no Attention and this leads to un-awareness.

Laban suggested these characteristics of the incomplete effort of Flow-Weight were representative of a **Dreamlike mode.**

**2a)** In this first example in the second pair of opposites, the emphasis is on motion factors Space and Flow, giving us information about Where and How.

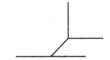

Graph Space and Flow Factors

**Space** (as in where) is related to Attention.

**i) Focus is centred on oneself.** As when a person is introverted and entirely concerned with his own predicament.

**ii) A general view of everything.** As when a theatre-goer looks around with universal attention before taking his seat.

**Flow** (as in how) is related to Precision.

**iii) Abandon.** As when a child hears some lively music and dances uninhibitedly.

**iv) Restraint.** As when a nurse dresses a very painful wound.

**Space-Flow.**

**v) A restrained general view of everything.** As when you are careful and cautious about possible eventualities and don't 'count your chickens before they're hatched.'

**vi) An abandoned view of everything.** As when everything seems to be wonderful, everybody is your friend and you are recklessly happy.

**vii) Focus on oneself with abandon.** As when you don't feel responsible for anyone, are answerable to no-one, and can therefore indulge recklessly in some forbidden pleasure.

**viii) Restrained focus on oneself.** As when an actor muses over the the good and bad points in his recent performance.

Without the Weight and Time factors relating to Intention and Decision, the attitude here is one of detachment.

Laban suggested the characteristics of the incomplete effort of Space-Flow were representative of a **Remote Mode**.

**2b)** In the second example of the second pair of opposites, the emphasis is on the motion factors Weight-Time, giving us information about What and When.

Graph Weight and Time Factors

**Weight** (as in what) is related to Intention.

**i) Strong attachment.** As when you have strong feelings for someone.

**ii) Lightness of touch.** As when you gently tease a friend.

**Time** (as in when) is related to Decision.

**iii) Emotional impact.** As when a husband tells his unsuspecting wife that he is leaving her for someone else.

**iv) Careful consideration.** As when reading the small print before signing a contract.

**Weight-Time.**

**v) Emotional impact with strong attachment.** As when falling in love.

**vi) Emotional impact and lightness of touch.** As when a young mother gives birth to a child and then holds it in her arms for the first time.

**vii) Careful consideration and strong attachment.** As when a loving friend is solicitous for your well-being but doesn't make it obvious.

**viii) Careful consideration and lightness of touch.** As when a surgeon takes time to plan a serious operation which he then performs with assured delicacy. The outstanding attitude is one of assurance. The missing motion factors are Space and Flow. Intention and Decision give the mover Presence, he has awareness and knows exactly what he is doing. Laban suggested the characteristics of the incomplete efforts of Weight-Time were expressive of a **Near Mode.**

**3a)** In this first pair of the third and last pair of opposites, the emphasis is on motion factors Space and Weight giving us information about Where and What.

Graph Space and Weight Factors

**Space** (as in where) is related to Attention.

**i) Focus may be powerfully direct.** As when a judge focuses powerfully on the face of a prisoner giving evidence.

**ii) Delicately flexible.** Like a bee going from flower to flower.

**Weight** (as in what) is related to Intention.

**iii) Stubbornly resolute.** As when you are determined to reach your goal, whatever the cost.

**iv) Sensitively receptive.** As when a student responds well to a teacher's advice.

**Space-Weight.**

**v) Powerfully direct focus and stubbornly resolute.** As when you know exactly what your goal is and will allow nothing to get in your way.

**vi) Powerfully direct focus and sensitively receptive.** As when you know exactly what your goal is but will respond willingly to any helpful advice.

**vii) Delicately flexible and stubbornly resolute.** As when you throw a dart. Physically, you are flexible, but mentally, you are determined to hit the bullseye.

**viii) Delicately flexible and sensitively receptive.** Both these qualities are in evidence when playing table tennis.

The predominant attitude is one of constancy, of steadfastness.

The motion factors Time and Flow are absent, and Attention and Intention combine instead.

Laban suggested the characteristics of the incomplete efforts of Space-Weight were representative of a **Stable Mode.**

**3b)** In this second pair of the third and final pair of opposites, the emphasis is on the motion factors Time and Flow, giving us information about When and How.

Graph Time and Flow Factors

**Time** (as in when) is related to Decision.

**i) Slowly forthcoming.** As when you are reluctant to impart information but in the end do so.

**ii) Abruptly changing.** As when you constantly change your mind.

**Flow** (as in how) is related to Precision.

**iii) Free, easy.** As when running down the stairs without a care.

**iv) Spasmodic, jerky.** As when walking on a stony beach with bare feet.

## Time-Flow

**v) Slowly forthcoming and easy progression.** As when you slowly recall memories from the past and enjoy telling them to willing listeners.

**vi) Slowly forthcoming and jerky.** A reluctance to impart information which comes in spasmodic bursts.

**vii) Abruptly changing with easy progression.** As when a consummate liar keeps changing his testimony with great ease.

**viii) Abruptly changing with jerky progression.** As when a perfectionist constantly rearranges items on display and is never satisfied.

The motion factors of Space and Weight are absent, meaning that Attention and Intention are not meaningful. There is a restlessness about Time-Flow which gives rise to adaptability of behaviour. Laban suggested the characteristics of the incomplete efforts of Time-Flow were representative of a **Mobile Mode**.

Attitudes, motion factors and elements are single units which build up collectively into groupings and, in so doing, each single constituent is completely submerged, resulting in the 'whole being larger than its parts', the whole grouping having a new meaning, importance and function not achieved by the individual units in themselves. Attitudes often have a recovery function, transitions between essential actions.

# 7

# *The Four Drives*

What is meant by a 'Drive'? It is believed that Laban did not just use the term in the way that psychologists use it, as a means of motivating behaviour, but also saw the Drives in terms of movement structure. Each Drive is a map in which different motion factors are combined; atoms of movements developing into molecular combinations which have four different characteristic behaviour patterns: Action, Vision, Spell and Passion Drives.

It is because of their intricate complexity that it is impossible to give precisely detailed analyses as easily as were given in the simpler incomplete efforts section. An attempt has been made, at the end of each Drive, to provide a scenario, in which some of the behavioural characteristics belonging to that particular Drive are incorporated.

The Drives, with their four recognisable types of behaviour, display an inexhaustible amount of movement patterns. It is inevitable that each Drive will have its own characteristics because each has its own mixture of motion factors and, taken as a whole, they have the possibility of covering the whole spectrum of movement behaviour.

*Laban explains the Drives thus: 'In considering the combination of the three motion factors, we arrive at a basic set of new variations. These are usually observed when the expression is more intense, more pronounced or more communicative than the display of inner attitudes.'*

## ACTION DRIVE

Three modes, one from each pair of opposite incomplete efforts, are unique to this Drive.

**Flow is latent**

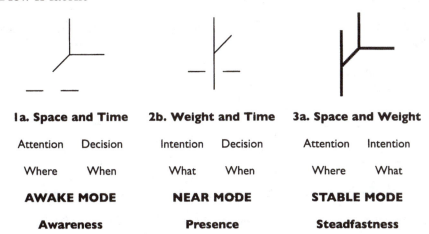

| **1a. Space and Time** | **2b. Weight and Time** | **3a. Space and Weight** |
|---|---|---|
| Attention    Decision | Intention    Decision | Attention    Intention |
| Where    When | What    When | Where    What |
| **AWAKE MODE** | **NEAR MODE** | **STABLE MODE** |
| **Awareness** | **Presence** | **Steadfastness** |

The variants of awareness, presence and steadfastness seem ideal constituents for working at routine tasks and also those of a repetitive nature. It is comprised of three concretely measurable components, namely, Space, Time and Weight, resulting in movements which are clear-cut in a purely functional manner. Shadow moves and conventional gestures may also occur.

**Vision, Spell** and **Passion Drives** cannot be so precisely determined as **Action Drive**. Man, unlike animals, can alter his movement patterns if he wishes. Working in a practical capacity, his bodily actions will be distinguished by his personal expressiveness. Even so, there may be times when his inner participation flags and the action appears mechanical. Alternatively, many rich and varied movement patterns can also arise, appearing to serve no practical purpose; these are the roots of his personality and manifest themselves in observable, characteristic, expressive behaviour.

Each of these three Drives has two modes in which Flow replaces Space, Time or Weight as a motion factor, relegating it to a latent place. The appearance of Flow gives rise to more expressive characteristics. However, there is one mode in each Drive that does not feature Flow.

Shadow movements and conventional gestures enrich individual behaviour, as we have observed.

## VISION DRIVE

Three modes, one from each pair of incomplete efforts, unique to this Drive.

**Weight is latent**

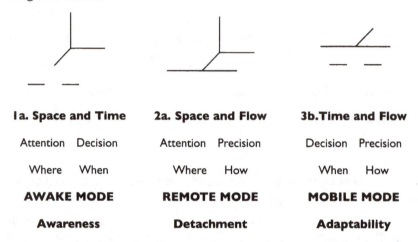

| 1a. Space and Time | 2a. Space and Flow | 3b. Time and Flow |
|:---:|:---:|:---:|
| Attention    Decision | Attention    Precision | Decision    Precision |
| Where    When | Where    How | When    How |
| **AWAKE MODE** | **REMOTE MODE** | **MOBILE MODE** |
| **Awareness** | **Detachment** | **Adaptability** |

Only the Awake Mode is comprised of two measurable components. The following scenario is an attempt to portray some of the behavioural characteristics of this Drive.

● It is a Saturday afternoon and the square is full of people enjoying themselves (Space and Flow) when a secret agent slowly (Time) and inconspicuously (Space) joins the throng. Finding a good vantage point in a shop doorway, he notices from his reflection in the glass that his hat is too far back on his head (Space). Quickly, he pulls it over his brow (Time). In his pocket he can feel the reassurance of a loaded revolver (Space and Flow). Suddenly, a crowd of jubilant football fans bursts into the square (Time and Flow), singing and shouting in celebration (Flow) of the match that their team has just won. The agent casts his eyes over the surging mob (Space), in the middle of which he can see the man (Space and Flow) he has been sent to eliminate. The fellow is well aware that he is a marked man but he is hopeful that the crowd will afford him anonymity (Flow and Space). Pretending to join in all the cheers and laughter (Time), he has a certain wary watchfulness about him (Space). All at once (Time), he recognises his would-be killer (Space, Time and Flow). Keeping up the pretence of jollity, he slackens his pace (Time) as he figures out what to do and, choosing his moment, turns and runs back the way he has come (Flow and Time), zig-zagging in and out of the remaining revellers. In a flash he has vanished (Time, Space and Flow). The agent curses the fact that once again he has been foiled (Flow).

## SPELL DRIVE

Three modes, one from each pair of opposite incomplete efforts, are unique to this Drive.

**Time is latent**

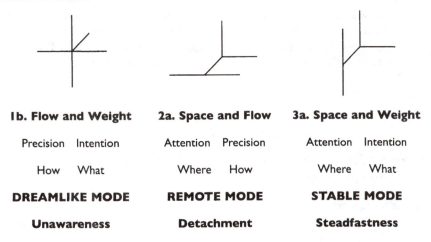

| **1b. Flow and Weight** | **2a. Space and Flow** | **3a. Space and Weight** |
|:---:|:---:|:---:|
| Precision   Intention | Attention   Precision | Attention   Intention |
| How   What | Where   How | Where   What |
| **DREAMLIKE MODE** | **REMOTE MODE** | **STABLE MODE** |
| **Unawareness** | **Detachment** | **Steadfastness** |

Only the Stable Mode is comprised of two measurable components. The following scenario is an attempt to portray some of the behavioural characteristics of this Drive.

● Annabelle is busy preparing for a dinner party that evening. She is a good cook and all that remains to be done is the elaborate dessert, a speciality of hers. This requires most of the rich ingredients to be put into the mixer. Having done this, she switches it on. Just at that moment, the phone rings and, rather unwisely, she answers it (Weight and Flow). It is her mother: half-an-hour later they are still talking (Weight and Flow). Ringing off, she remembers that the mixer is still churning her precious dessert. To her horror, the whole mixture has become a useless, noxious mess (Weight, Flow and Space). Distraught, poor Annabelle rings her best friend (Weight and Flow) Daphne, for advice. Daphne, who will be a guest at the dinner party, offers to make another dessert and bring it round before the other guests arrive. Annabelle is overwhelmingly relieved and grateful (Weight, Space and Flow). Daphne arrives with a dessert that is even more spectacular than Annabelle's would have been (Weight and Flow). The dinner party goes with a swing and the main courses have been much appreciated, but everyone is waiting for the spectacular dessert (Weight and Flow). After refilling her guests' glasses, Annabelle goes to the kitchen to fetch it. Should she tell the guests that Daphne has made it? (Weight) No, she thinks (Weight and Flow). Perhaps later on. Triumphantly, she comes in holding it aloft and strikes a pose (Flow, Space and Weight). Everyone applauds, including Daphne. Annabelle then advances towards the table, still holding the dessert aloft. She is just about to place it on the table when she trips on the edge of the carpet (or was it Daphne's foot?) and falls headlong, sending the delicious dessert all over the guests (Space, Flow and Weight).

## PASSION DRIVE

Three modes, one from each pair of opposite incomplete efforts, are unique to this Drive.

**Space is latent**

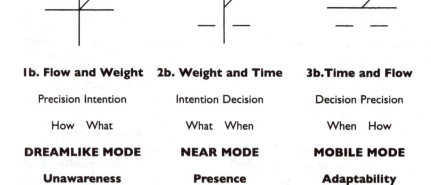

| 1b. Flow and Weight | 2b. Weight and Time | 3b. Time and Flow |
|---|---|---|
| Precision Intention | Intention Decision | Decision Precision |
| How    What | What    When | When    How |
| **DREAMLIKE MODE** | **NEAR MODE** | **MOBILE MODE** |
| **Unawareness** | **Presence** | **Adaptability** |

Only the Near Mode is comprised of two measurable components. The following scenario is an attempt to portray some of the behavioural characteristics of this Drive.

● The actor peers through a hole in the curtain at the audience taking their seats in the auditorium. Being a matinee, he is delighted to see that the house is full (Weight and Flow). Returning thoughtfully to his dressing room (Time), he goes through some of his more difficult lines carefully (Flow). Looking at his reflection in the mirror, he is not at all satisfied with the knotted scarf around his neck (Weight) and quickly (Time and Flow) re-arranges it. Finally satisfied, he takes one last look in the mirror, before walking quietly (Time and Flow) to the wings of the stage. Concentrating on his part (Flow) he waits patiently for his entrance (Time). Hearing his cue (Flow and Weight), he strides onto the stage and mounts a platform in order to address an assembly of bedraggled labourers in a rousing speech that is the highlight of the play (Weight, Time and Flow). His voice resounds throughout the theatre, at times, angry at their acceptance of their lot and urging them to rise in protest against the dictator who makes their lives such a misery (Weight and Flow). His voice then becomes warm and sympathetic when he describes the wretched conditions they are expected to endure (Time, Weight and Flow). It is a magnetic performance. The tirade lasts for twenty minutes until news comes of the approach of the secret police (Time, Weight and Flow). The heroic speaker shows no fear (Weight), but his faithful band of followers hustle him away to safety (Time) as the curtain falls to the rapturous applause of the audience (Weight). The actor returns to his dressing room, bathed in perspiration. Dragging off his uncomfortably wet ragged scarf (Weight and Flow), he wipes himself with a dry towel before slumping into his chair (Time, Weight and Flow) to await the evening performance where he has to do it all again.

Note there are many more variations than those selected, in the three scenarios mentioned above. Do not despair! As someone said, 'Drives should come with a health warning!'.

Laban spent a life-time observing and analysing human movement. He encouraged his students to sharpen their powers of observation and would regularly send them to local thoroughfares to 'use their eyes'. From watching people going about their business in the street to relaxing at parties, whether singly or in groups, one can begin to recognise behaviour patterns, shadow movements, incomplete efforts and even gain an insight into Drives.

## THE MEANING OF MUSIC

The word 'music' comes from the Greek and literally means 'the art of the muse' and, thus, it implied 'the fine art that is concerned with the combination of sounds with a view to beauty of form and the expression of thought or feeling.' This is a very elevated view of music that would seem to exclude folk music and the vast variety of popular music.

Music means different things to different people if, indeed, it 'means' anything at all. It can range from a few disparate notes, as from an idly plucked guitar, to something highly structured, as in the works of Johann Sebastian Bach. With the idly plucked notes, where there is no intended 'meaning', the hearer (rather than the listener) may find that the rise and fall of certain tones will touch some hidden chord deep in his psyche so that, to him, there *is* meaning. With music such as Bach's, the listener (rather than the hearer) can recognise the structure of the sounds which have been ordered into melodic and rhythmic patterns and shapes that somehow give it logic and meaning.

There is a considerable difference in hearing and listening; hearing is passive and listening is active. For instance, it is possible to listen intently but not hear intently. Also, people hear and listen in different ways. One can hear music and not be involved in it; it acts merely as a background to whatever has a prior claim to our attention. To listen to music requires a definite involvement, whether readily, on our part, or in spite of ourselves. Listening, is to follow the course the composer (if there is one) has set down for us. All good compositions have a logical follow-through, or pathway, that is quite as compelling as a good story, so that we do not wish to miss any part of it. Music without a composer, such as traditional music that has been handed down, can be equally appealing to the hearer and compelling to the listener, though the meaning will be less clear. Nature has many musical sounds to offer which are pleasing to hear, such as the babbling of a brook, or the wind in the trees. These do not have meaning except that we know what is causing the sound, which is pleasing and can lull our senses. Likewise, birdsong. We can be enchanted by the blackbird's mellifluous outpourings but we do not know what it means. Presumably he does. All we know is that it is lovely, and in his note patterns and intervals we find our own meanings which is what we do with most of the music we listen to.

There are three major components in music: melody, harmony and time. The earliest music consisted only of a single line of notes that were sung or played that comprised a 'tune' of sorts. Later it was discovered that certain notes and, indeed certain clusters of notes, blended with the melody, and so harmony was discovered. Harmony consists of layers of notes which we call chords which are divided into two categories, concords and discords. A concord, when heard, leaves the ear satisfied that it does not need to 'move on', whereas a discord leaves the listener with the feeling that it needs to resolve itself. It should be pointed out that discords are not necessarily unpleasant as the name would imply. Often they are most attractive but they don't sound like an end in themselves. The third element is that of time, which includes rhythm, and refers to the *duration* of notes; this can be an entirely free rhythm, depending on the words sung or the instrument played, or it can be a regular, metrical rhythm.

Music embodies many other disciplines. These include Mathematics, Architecture, Balance, Proportion, Form, Physics, Law, Reason and Logic. Where ensemble playing is concerned, it is the perfect example of teamwork – better, it has to be said, than in sport because the aim is not to compete and win but to work together to achieve as perfect a rendition as possible. Balance of forces and light and shade are important factors of music-making that are equally applicable to how we should live. As such, it should be a major priority in education. It goes hand in hand with literature in songs and operas; a great deal of it induces movement, from foot-tapping to marching and dancing. It can soothe the weary spirit or it can rouse the torpid to a frenzy.

Most people will say they like some sort of music but there have been some individuals who claimed not to like it at all. Winston Churchill, reportedly didn't, and Ivy Compton Burnett, the acerbic novelist of dynastic upheavals, said she 'didn't see the point of it'. People respond to music in different ways: some respond to melody (a 'good tune'), while others respond more to rhythm. Music that appeals to the intellect, or that is deeply spiritual or highly emotional, is less reliant on rhythm, certainly as far as a regular beat is concerned. Indeed, the more regular the beat and the stronger it becomes, the more the music moves down from our higher, aesthetic sensibilities to our basic instincts; feet will tap and hips will indulge in sexy movements. Popular music has always relied on a regular beat, from early jazz and swing, through rock-and roll to the hard-rock of today, with its immense thumping, which is not aesthetic and doesn't claim to be.

Music has the advantage of being an international language though, its identity can be as varied as the countries it represents. We in Europe and the so-called West are used to the music of equal temperament (pioneered by Bach in 'The Well-Tempered Clavichord') where the natural tones of the Harmonic Series are strait-jacketed into octaves of twelve equal semi-tones. This is very different from the looser and freer tones of Arabic and Oriental music or the sounds still made by primitive tribes.

That music has meaning is fairly evident. In former ages, when music was not so continuously available, a few notes could mean a lot, as Shakespeare makes clear in several of his plays. In the early days before polyphony (that is, music of several harmonic layers) notes would be heard singly and the rise and fall of certain intervals would provoke a significant but inexplicable response which could be purely cerebral or clearly emotional. When Orsino says in his opening speech in *Twelfth Night*, 'That strain again! – it had a dying fall', it says volumes about the power of music. There are so many wonderful instances where Shakespeare uses or comments on the tremendous potency of music.

The trouble with music today is that there is too much of it! Since the advent of recording, there is more music filling the air than ever before in the history of mankind – much of it unwanted and much of it not listened to. Quite often it is inappropriate to the situation, the location, and the time of day. Indian music is much more specific when it comes to time of day; there they have particular arrangements of notes and melodic patterns, called ragas, for each three-hour section of the day, starting with Dawn. Very civilised. But music is universal; it can mean anything we want it to mean. It can be sad, it can be merry; it can be serious, it can be humorous; it can be harmonious, it can be discordant; it can be cool, it can be passionate; certainly music can seem to speak; often a phrase seems to ask a question and the following phrase will answer it. Music can also transform; the most tragic utterance can become beautiful when sung. So many of Schubert's wonderful songs are about unrequited love and many of them are pervaded with the ever-threatening approach of death (which came all too soon for him) yet they are all beautiful and, in a strange way, uplifting. When Purcell's stricken Dido sings 'When I am laid in earth,' you don't think 'What a miserable, depressing song,' you are carried away by the beauty of it. And music can make us dance – or want to! We might want to leap up and spin around or just sit and tap our feet but we want to dance!

## Playing Musical Instruments

Musical instruments are rather like sleeping creatures waiting for that magical moment that will bring them to life. In this case, the magical moment is when some sort of movement is applied to them: Stringed instruments are waiting to be plucked or have bows drawn across them, wind instruments are waiting for the movement of breath or air to pass through them, keyboard instruments are waiting for fingers to press their keys and feet to press their pedals, while percussion instruments are waiting to be tapped or banged or shaken. All these movements we can apply with ease, provided we are content with one or two notes, but

to go any further is to raise the question of technique, and to learn the technique of an instrument is to embark on a commitment akin to a love affair.

The shape of musical instruments is dictated by the levels of pitch they produce. The Greeks demonstrated the precept that 'the shorter the length, the higher the pitch' which explains the shape of the harp, the harpsichord and the grand piano. Length also applies to wind instruments – the longer and wider the tube, the lower the pitch; compare the tiny piccolo with the bass tuba or trombone. The pipes of the organ also show us how they increase in size and length as they get lower. Although the strings of the violin are all equal in length, as are those of the viola, cello, double-bass and guitar, their lower strings are thicker. Stretching these strings to a certain tension gives them their fundamental pitch; shortening the strings to make them higher is done with the player's fingers. Thus, the string player is particularly conscious of the equation of tension and pitch.

Most musical instruments are beautiful in shape and require beautiful movements to play them; the co-ordination of mind and body should match the instrument.

Choosing to play an instrument is to choose a partner, a partner to which our mind and body can respond. The physical aspect is important: the posture for playing the violin is quite different from the posture for playing the cello, and the player must be able to move comfortably in that posture. Similarly, the sideways position of playing the transverse flute may not suit some people as well as the forward hold of the oboe or clarinet. Every instrument needs ease of movement that suits the player. Ask yourself whether you would get more satisfaction out of tinkling a triangle or giving a bass drum a hell of a thump. If you are a person of contrasts you might like both!

Just as so many would-be dancers, who can happily improvise their own steps, lose courage when they actually have to *learn* steps (which requires technique), so it is with many would-be players of musical instruments – the initial enthusiasm is quick to wear off when it is realised that a great deal of practice has to be done to acquire any skill. We have already mentioned that any skill depends upon using the right muscles at the right time but there is more to it than that. To be skilled is to have a clear mental picture of the necessary pathways, and to use the right efforts to follow them. This is particularly relevant to playing a musical instrument where success is guaranteed if the right amount of effort is used – no more and no less – and at the right time – neither before or after. Stiffness occurs when the effort is too strong for the task in hand, or when it is not at the right time. Wrong notes occur when the effort is in the wrong place. What is important is what happens *between* the notes; playing a note is an *effort* after which, as Laban would say, there should be *recovery* – a much better word than relaxation – otherwise elasticity is forfeited. So, the playing of a musical instrument requires effort – to be precise, many different efforts: some strong, and some as light as a feather, from each of which there must be recovery! That is why we practise slowly.

There can be few human beings who do not get some pleasure out of touching a musical instrument to see how it works and what sort of sound it makes, but the thought of actually playing it is rather more daunting. Children are particularly curious and particularly responsive: set them loose in a room full of musical instruments and they will have a field day plucking and blowing and banging. But how not to lose that initial enthusiasm? Few children can withstand the manifold distractions of the media-orientated world of today in order to spend precious hours learning scales, arpeggios and countless exercises without any particular goal in sight. The whole thing becomes boring. A great deal of responsibility lies with the teacher, who should never let the learning process be reduced to a dull routine. It should be an exciting adventure, always seeking and finding and moving on. Studying with Laban was always an adventure. He encouraged us to seek and find out about the movement of our bodies, at the same time linking it with our mental faculties.

When Laban stresses the importance of the unity of the mind and the body, this is nowhere more apparent than in the string player who uses a bow. Let us observe the violinist: on the one side he holds the violin and on the other side he holds the bow. In between is his mind that will decide how to bring these two elements together. A good violinist knows in advance just how much pressure to give the bow in order to bring a string to life. At the same time, he knows by feel and by sense exactly what pitch these strings will produce. This is remarkable in that the violin, unlike the guitar, has no frets in order to guide the fingers. So, the violinist is playing what he *thinks* and what he *feels*. The same applies, of course, to the viola, cello and double-bass.

Most of us have an aptitude for certain skills but not others; this is something innate in our makeup. Some enviable individuals show this aptitude at a very early age and are able to excel at this skill having never been taught. The child prodigy is a case in point and is a supreme example of free-flow; there is no hang-up, no hesitation; the individual knows instinctively what pathways to take and what efforts to use and does so with confidence.

Now, for those of you who fell by the wayside with your early musical studies and who can be heard saying: 'I wish I hadn't given it up as I would so like to be able to play,' all is not lost. Look around the room you are in at the moment and see how many objects you can find that can produce a sound. There are the obvious things like vases, bowls and drinking glasses which, when tapped, may reward your ears with actual notes, but other interesting sounds can be found by tapping various surfaces, hollow boxes and tins. Also, shaking tins of pins is a good substitute for maracas; plucking stretched rubber-bands can produce different pitches, while cutlery items can produce a wealth of interesting sounds.

All this shows us how we are surrounded by the possibility of many fascinating sounds which, if harnessed, can be a wonderfully effective accompaniment to dance. A small group of enthusiasts can provide a spontaneous orchestra which can either follow the dancers by mirroring the movements in sound, or it can build up sound pictures in advance which the dancers can follow.

# 8

## *For Those Who Act*

Actors have been described as making a living by pretending to be someone else. However, acting is not the preserve of just actors; every one of us acts at some time or other but not necessarily on the stage. We often have to act when we are not pleased to see somebody but must give the impression we are pleased to see them. The business man doing the hard sell is acting; doctors frequently act to their patients; politicians are acting all the time, while lawyers make a very profitable living out of acting. All these people are trying to sound convincing, saying things they do not necessarily mean. Some are better than others at this. With them, though, it is not an art form, whereas to the professional actor, sounding convincing and, in fact, *being* convincing in the character he is playing is a major part of his skill. As for pretending to be someone else, this is not always the case. More and more, since the advent of television, actors are required to play themselves or, at least, extensions of themselves.

Television acting, and the fast bucks it affords, not to mention voice-overs and commercials, have succeeded in obscuring the importance of even the most basic stage movement and the importance of voices that can fill a large theatre. This fact has been lamentably obvious when certain television stars take to the stage and promptly lose their voices. Their sense of movement also is often exposed as woefully inadequate.

An actor needs to be able to use his body like an instrument so that he can move with majestic grace or, if need be, rank clumsiness, according to the character he is playing. He should be able to project any physical or emotional state by the way he moves and the way he speaks. Thus, he needs to know how his physical state can be affected by fatigue, illness, pain, fear, nerves, being too hot or too cold, being inebriated or under the influence of drugs. Likewise, he needs to know how his feelings and emotions can be affected by happiness, misery, ecstasy, grief, hatred, love, jealousy, anger, hysteria from either joy or grief and many other similar influences. Having done this, he should be able to recreate any of these states and project it to an audience.

An actor must also consider his costume very carefully. If he is in a period play, he must know how to move in the clothes as though he really *does* wear them every day. Sleeves will greatly affect the movement of the arms just as skirts will affect walking. Sometimes a costume demands to be shown off, be it lace cuffs or a magnificent train and, of course, the manners and gestures must reflect the period. The shoes, also, play an important part, for they will affect the way an actor walks; the high heels of the Restoration period will feel quite different from, say, the flat winkle-pickers of Medieval times.

An actor needs to be able to react to his imagined environment. Battling against a gale force wind is very different from having it at his back. Walking through mud, or deep snow or fallen leaves will each have a particular movement characteristic. So will walking on ice which may hold or may give way at any moment. So will walking on roasting hot sand or sharp pebbles. These are all images he can picture and re-create so that the audience can *feel* it.

Like anyone else, actors have their natural movement preferences which may or may not suit the character they are playing. By extending their range of movement they will open up immense possibilities of playing many diverse roles. Similarly, the voice should be extended in range and flexibility so that, apart form being audible, it becomes a sensitive instrument that can convey any physical or emotional state.

The importance of breathing needs hardly to be stressed to the actor, and this is not just a question of being able to take a good breath and controlling it for vocal purposes, but of knowing how to *use* that breath to convey emotion. Running out of breath is always a worry but *using* it, whether you run out of it or not, is far more vital.

We have observed how the emotions affect our breathing and, for the actor, it is a stimulating and reassuring exercise to consider various emotions purely in terms of breathing. Think how you breathe when you are angry and how differently you breathe when you are contented; think how you breathe when you are grief-stricken and how differently you breathe when you are blissfully happy. Run through as many emotions as you can think of – happiness, misery, ecstasy, grief, etc. – purely in terms of breathing then, when you are studying a part, you should find it very beneficial and illuminating to go through it purely in terms of breathing. Take Hamlet, for example; his breathing will be different in nearly every scene, according to his disposition. As for Othello, his breathing will change radically when his jealousy is aroused.

## Using the Eight Basic Efforts to Convey Character

Before launching into anything extensive, let us see how the eight Basic Efforts can effect the voice:

- Take the word, 'Yes', and say it in a Gliding manner. Give yourself time to think what Gliding is and apply it to your voice. Then try saying 'Yes' in the manner of Floating, Dabbing, Flicking, Wringing, Pressing, Thrusting and Slashing. You can do them in any order you prefer but make sure you have it clearly in your mind which Effort you are about to do. They should all sound quite different, as 'yes' often does in conversation. However, do take particular care to differentiate between Gliding and Floating, Dabbing and Flicking, Wringing and Pressing, and Thrusting and Slashing.

- Try the same process on the word, 'No', and any other everyday monosyllables you can think of. Follow this with a variety of words and phrases from daily life, such as: Really? How nice. I think so. I know. Leave it to me. No problem, etc.

Using the eight Basic Efforts can be very helpful where sub-text acting is required, that is saying one thing but meaning another. A charming example of this is when a girl says to her caressing boyfriend, 'Don't,' when he knows perfectly well she means, 'Carry on!'

- Try saying 'I hate you!' But *mean* 'I love you!' This is a fairly common practice. Less common and more difficult is to say, 'I love you!' and really mean, 'I hate you!'

Actors are well known for meeting somebody they detest and saying, 'Darling, how lovely to see you!' but we all say similar things to a greater or lesser degree.

- Try saying a phrase in a Gliding manner but *feel* you would rather be Slashing.

- Try saying a phrase in a Floating manner and *feel* you would rather be Pressing.

- Try saying a phrase in a Dabbing manner but *feel* you would rather be Thrusting.

- Try saying a phrase in a Flicking manner but *feel* you would rather be Wringing.

From all this, it can be seen that consciously using one Basic Effort and applying it to a speech can entirely change the character of the speech. Sometimes the Effort will be appropriate, sometimes not. Either way, it will help you find the right direction for the character you are playing. The piece may demand a bravado performance, but trying it through in, say, a Floating manner or, indeed, all of the Basic Effort characteristics, should strengthen your conviction of how it *should* be done.

- Take a short speech from a play, or a piece of poetry or prose, and read it out loud in the way you think it should be done. It is a good idea to record yourself doing this, and what ensues. Now, read the piece through in a Gliding manner, followed by the other seven Efforts: Floating, Dabbing, Flicking, Wringing, Pressing, Thrusting and Slashing, changing the order as you wish. Finally, read the piece through, again, as you think it should be done and compare it with your first attempt. There should be a considerable difference. Listen, of course, to all your versions; you can learn much from this.

### *Improvisation Exercise using One Effort Only*

The characters do not touch each other at any time. They must command the space in between each other. Imagine that a bank manager has advertised for a private secretary and the first applicant is waiting outside his door to be interviewed. Both characters are only permitted to use one effort each throughout the improvisation. In this instance, the applicant may only use a **Floating** effort and the bank manager may only use a **Thrusting** effort. Remember this is a movement exercise with speech, and is a test at how good you are at sustaining one effort only over a period of time.

## *Applicant*

- From the moment you enter, you must give a **Floating** perform-ance. The distance to the manager or a chair may be quite a long one. You will not know exactly because you will not have a concen-trated, direct focus. Indeed your pathway will be circuitously flexible and sustained, your focus indirect and glancing. With your sustained, light and flexible movement, you may 'locomote' any way that feels right for this effort. This also applies to use of a table or chair, for example, **Floating** over, under, round or on it. Breathe comfortably and only speak when you are ready for your voice to accommodate your **Floating** movement.

Of course, in everyday life one is not confined to one effort. We are using a variety of effort changes continually, constantly adapting to our needs. These exercises help the actor to extend his movement range by concentrating on one effort only and sustaining it against a fellow actor working on a different effort.

## *Bank Manager*

- From the moment the applicant enters you are ready to conduct a **Thrusting** interview; in other words, you are in charge and conscious of time. Your actions are strong, sudden and direct and this is clearly demonstrated in your personal behaviour and the familiarity with which you move around your office and the position of the furniture (if any). You want to know the sort of person he/she is and their work experience to date in the shortest possible time.

As you already know, **Floating** and **Thrusting** are in opposition, at opposite ends of the same diagonal. It is often a question of luck when you are asked to try out a certain effort. If you are given one that you are comfortable with, you will probably sustain its rhythm throughout. If it is one that you find difficult, there is a danger that you will end up changing to the other person's effort rhythm. Often characters using a **Thrusting** effort get so irritated by characters using a **Floating** effort that they want to take hold of them in order to get their attention. That is failure.

- Try again with the same bank manager as the **Floater** and the same applicant as the **Thruster**.

- Change over roles and try both efforts in your new characters.
- Imagine a dry cleaning service and a dissatisfied customer whose favourite evening dress has been ruined.

*Other examples:*

- A waiter and a diner.
- A gardener and house-owner.
- A newly married couple on their honeymoon.

You will have ideas of your own. Try out all the efforts singly, not necessarily completely contrasting ones.

Note that working on single efforts does not produce 'real life' acting, simply because, as you already know, we do not remain locked into one effort. However, it is quite amazing how much we learn from the characters' efforts and movement pathways. We get an insight into their feelings.

- Bring others into the scene with their effort. At the call, 'Change' everyone switches to a predetermined new effort and continues the scene without pausing.

*Improvisation using Multiple Efforts*

- Imagine holding a conversation whilst standing up and exchanging places in a rowing boat. How would you simulate the rocking boat in terms of effort? What efforts would you use in the improvisation and how would they affect your voice?
- Try a similar situation on a liner. Heavy seas are making a promenade on the deck difficult.
- You are on a fractious horse waiting for the starting signal. Can you simulate the bodily reactions to the horse's skittish behaviour?
- Imagine you are walking on a parapet.
- Holding a helium balloon, you are suddenly airborne.
- Skating on an ice rink as i) an accomplished skater or ii) beginner.

## *Character Improvisation*

● Imagine a council meeting of residents of a picturesque village. A cross section of the community, they share a desire to improve the community even if they are not always agreed on the way ahead. For instance, will the building of new houses improve the village or spoil it? Should the increasing traffic through the village be endured or is the proposed by-pass across valuable pasture a better alternative?

In a group improvisation, the participents should decide what sort of character they are playing; what sort of efforts they would use and how these choices would affect their behaviour. There would be obvious distinctions of class and wealth.

This type of improvisation really needs someone outside to intercede when necessary. For example, if an actor dries up and finds he is losing his character, he should come out and watch the action. He will probably be stimulated and find that he wants to return later and should do so.

It is worth noting that the improvisations between two people were concerned with maintaining one effort throughout; care had to be taken not to be influenced by the other person's effort rhythm. In the group improvisation, the actor has more recourse to the full range of efforts, selecting what is necessary for his character. It is assumed that some of the group will be more familiar with certain characters than others, knowing how they will behave, whilst others may be complete strangers.

## Using the Incomplete Efforts, Modes and Drives

### Movement Improvisation

Perhaps the most difficult concept for actors, who depend on language to express themselves, is to realise that there are many more movements than there are words to decribe them. This is particularly the case when attempting to come to terms with all the innumerable variations contained in the Modes and Drives. However, the technique can be learnt and used with great effect.

In the chapter on Incomplete Efforts, we described the different types of behaviour that would possibly result from different pairs of opposites.

We also know that when Flow replaces a motion factor, feelings are heightened. The shapes of our movement pathways reflect our moods, resulting in increasingly dynamic, rhythmic behaviour when movement sensation takes over from objective function. This is particularly so in Vision, Spell and Passion Drives when a welter of emotions are surging through the 'character'.

One should be aware of the different expressions Laban has used in an effort to be as precise as possible but do not be overwhelmed by them! Go for the movement technique and the characteristics associated with each attitude.

### Using Space

### Where

Where do you place your **Attention**? Do you focus on a particular person or object in a direct, concentrated way or glance around, in a flexible manner, taking in a more general view of your surroundings?

- Try focusing on yourself. Look at your clothes, your body and limbs, the contents of your pockets and your bag. Be immersed in yourself; even using mirrors to see how you look from either side or from behind.

- Focus your attention on an object. Examine every detail of it, observing from the High, Medium and Deep zones, both close to you and from afar. Do not concern yourself with anything else.

- Focus on a mass of people milling about in the distance – either real or imaginary. Do not pick out any individuals but try and be aware of the movement pattern as a whole.

- Focus on one person in the moving mass of people. Walk in different directions to keep this person in sight, sometimes hurrying, sometimes pausing. You could, for instance, imagine you were looking back over your shoulder to see if a friend was trying to catch up with you.

- Can you focus on the wall tapestry high above you? Is that your cottage you can see down in the valley? Try looking into the distance with half-closed eyes. Relax your focus and allow a more hazy or diffused view to appear, in strong contrast to the focused images.

216

## Using Time

### When

When do you make your **Decision**?

● Imagine you are suddenly awakened from a deep sleep by the sound of breaking glass. You immediately decide to go and investigate.

● Now, in contrast, imagine that you have a very serious decision to make affecting the rest of your life. It requires you to reflect carefully in a sustained manner before you commit yourself to a life-changing situation.

## Using Weight

### What

What is your **Intention**? Is it light-hearted, sensitively pin-pointing or exalted? Or do you have a weighty, heavy or gloomy intention? How does your bodily movement change with each of these attitudes?

● Do you strongly intend to post that important letter before the last collection?

● Or is your intention rather light-hearted, so that missing the collection does not worry you? This would suggest that you didn't rate posting it on time very highly, seemingly, the wrong attitude for such an important letter.

● 'You must come to dinner!' A genuine invitation, seriously intended at the time. But the days pass and you begin to have misgivings. It would be rather expensive and, anyway, you have so little time. It is really a bit of a bother. Perhaps, they have forgotten all about the invitation? The once-firm intention has now become rather superficial in your mind. (If your acquaintances ring to confirm a date, you may well go ahead with gloomy intention!)

## Using Flow

### How

With what **Precision** do you use your Flow? When Flow replaces one of the three motion factors, feelings are heightened. It is the precision with which we complete a task. It can happen in a free-flowing, pouring out, abandoned fashion or be held back, restrained, suggesting a much more cautious approach. It can also become jerky, as in letting go and then pausing.

- The gifted violinist is 'giving his all'. The audience is enthralled, listening to the outpouring of music and emotion, recognising the artist's love for his craft.

- The beginner, learning to play his instrument, handles it a little awkwardly and experiments with the bow moving over the strings, unsure of what sounds will greet his ears. His cautious, rather controlled, approach restrains his Flow.

**Using the Awake Mode**

**Attention** (Where in Space) **and Decision** (When in Time)

This is the first of the first pair of opposites, as shown in the Incomplete Efforts diagram on page 189. When our bodily actions demonstrate incomplete effort participation, they disclose a variety of Inner Attitudes. In this mode, whether one is certain or uncertain in these situations, the inner attitude displays the characteristic behaviour of **Awareness.**

- In the middle of the night, you are sudenly awakened by the sound of someone breaking in. You sit bolt upright as you listen for further sounds before you decide what to do.

- Disturbed by a sound in the middle of the night, you creep downstairs in a restrained manner to investigate.

- Hearing the sound of a traffic accident outside your house, you rush downstairs and out into the street to see if you can be of any help.

- Coming round from an operation, you open your eyes gradually and view your familiar surroundings hazily.

- You are in a beautiful garden. Gradually accustoming yourself to the fading light, you attempt to capture all the sights and sounds and the exotic smells and perfumes that surround you.

## Using the Dream Mode

**Precision** (How in Flow) and **Intention** (What in Weight)

This mode is paired with the Awake mode. Flow now replaces another motion factor and gives rise to more expressive feelings, emotions playing a stronger part. The inner attitude displays the characteristic behaviour of **Unawareness.**

- Highly pleased at passing all your exams, you want to rush out excitedly to tell everyone, and to celebrate.

- Having failed miserably in your exams, your attitude is one of gloomy despair and you wallow in self-pity.

- Your exam results are excellent and you feel absolutely exalted about your future opportunities as a brain surgeon, but you are guarded about mentioning it to anyone.

- Your exam results are pretty dreadful but somehow, you feel that you might still become a brain surgeon.

## Using the Remote Mode

**Attention** (Where in Space) and **Precision** (How in Flow)

This is the first of the second pair of opposites as shown in the Incomplete Efforts diagram on page 191. This mode is paired with the Near mode. Flow now replaces another motion factor and gives rise to more expressive feelings, emotions playing a stronger part. Intention (Weight) and Decision (Time) are latent, resulting in the inner attitude displaying the characteristic behaviour of **Detachment.**

- Before you, down an incline, lies a vast expanse of smooth lawn which fills you with elation. Taking a deep breath of pleasure, you rush down into the middle of it and exult in the space.

- You are focusing on your feet as you walk gingerly down a very muddy bank.

- You focus on a tree in the distance and race towards it as fast as you can.

- You are walking in a crowded street. Vaguely aware of the bustle and noise, you walk on in a restrained manner.

## Using the Near Mode

**Intention** (What in Weight) and **Decision** (When in Time)

This completes the second pair of opposites as shown in the Incomplete Efforts diagram on page 192. Flow and Space are latent, resulting in the inner attitude displaying the characteristic behaviour of **Presence.**

- Your new colleague in the office has arrived. You have every intention of treating her warmly, making for a strong working relationship.

- You have decided to treat your new colleague in a rather casual way but are willing to give her any assistance when she needs it.

- You don't like the new arrival's over familiar manner so you suddenly decide to be rather aloof.

- Your secretary's strong feelings for you, sustained over a period of time, are suddenly irresistible.


## Using the Stable Mode

**Attention** (Where in Space) and **Intention** (What in Weight)

This is the first of the last pair of opposites as shown in the Incomplete Efforts diagram on page 193. Flow and Time are latent, making the inner attitude behaviour characteristic of **Steadfastness.**

- You are a celebrated rose expert and are enjoying identifying the perfumes of your favourite specimens.

- You encounter a rose you can't identify but are overwhelmed by its powerful and distinctive perfume.

- A child handles a rose with delicate flexibility to avoid the thorns and sensitively smells its fragrance.

- A fractious little boy struggles to escape from restraining arms. Breaking free, he immediately falls into the pond.

## Using the Mobile Mode

**Decision** (When in Time) and **Precision** (How in Flow)

This last mode is paired with the stable mode.

The characteristic of this mode is **Adaptability**.

- In the train, a young man is chatting up the young girl opposite him with practised charm. She is unimpressed and attempts to ignore his remarks.

- Changing his approach, he tries a more flippant line of approach, still confident that he can score.

- The girl becomes increasingly fed-up and decides to move to another seat.

- The easy chat is halted as it dawns on the young Lothario that it is not welcome.

- As she leaves the train, the girl, accidentally-on-purpose, treads on the young man's foot with one of her stiletto shoes.

## Using the Four Drives

In the Incomplete Efforts, we have noticed that one motion factor is latent and only two (of which Flow may be one) give expression to the movement. However, when Flow combines with **two** other motion factors, making three active, as is the case in the Drives, the expression is 'more intense, more pronounced and more communicative than in the display of inner attitudes'.

### Action Drive

Space, Time and Weight are contained in this Drive, Flow is latent. Objective function (Attention, Intention and Decision) enables a task to be carried through efficiently without any particular 'feelings' affecting the movement.

- Cleaning your teeth.
- Planting seedlings.
- Working as a typist.

*Vision Drive*

In Vision Drive, Flow replaces Weight. Virtually lacking Intention, behaviour becomes Vision-like. The modes which do not feature Weight are:

Awake (Space and Time), Remote (Space and Flow) and Mobile (Time and Flow). Each of the three modes has been worked through separately; now they synthesise in Vision Drive and emotional behaviour is heightened. Almost without Weight, without Intention, playing a central part in this Drive, emotional feelings are related to spatial shape and to Flow.

The variants are endless. You could use these modes separately and then try combining them and, perhaps, finding your own words to express your resulting behaviour.

*Spell Drive*

In Spell Drive, Flow replaces Time. Virtually lacking the ability to make Decisions, behaviour becomes Spell-like. The three modes which do not feature Time are:

Dreamlike (Flow and Weight), Remote (Space and Flow), Stable (Space and Weight). Almost without Time, without Decision, a person in this Drive appears less concerned with immediate action, feelings taking on the characteristic behaviour of someone in a trance, or mesmerised.

Work through as for Vision Drive, trying the modes separately before attempting to put them together.

*Passion Drive*

In Passion Drive, Flow replaces Space. Virtually lacking Attention, the three modes that do not feature Space are:

Dreamlike (Flow and Weight), Near (Weight and Time) and Mobile (Time and Flow).

In this Drive, there is virtually no Attention to Space and shapes and probably, therefore, the person is unaware of his dynamic movement pathways resulting from his mood. The central attitude is one of Intention, of concern for one's own feelings. Perhaps this person is 'wrapped up in himself'.

*Note:* Another way of trying out the Drives is to start with Action Drive, move to transitional Incomplete efforts and then attempt to go into one of the three Drives having Flow as a constituent.

## COMMEDIA DELL'ARTE

Laban's effort studies are excellent material for establishing the movement behaviour of the characters from the commedia dell'arte. The 'functional' actions of what is called their 'physicality' are clearly displayed through the use of Basic Efforts which define the qualities of the characters.

The origins of the commedia dell'arte began some eight centuries before Christ when a band of comic actors wandered throughout Greece performing comedies with music. It was not long before other bands developed more ambitious programmes such as spectacles mixing dancing, burlesque and pantomimes. The performers were also acrobats, tumblers and tight-rope walkers, skilled at improvisation. Women were an integral part of the cast, some of their major roles ranking as highly as those of their male colleagues. Families would hand down roles from one generation to the next and, as a result, their amateur status evolved to a more professional one. Spreading to Rome and beyond, the commedia dell'arte was often much preferred to the classic theatre of the day.

Through the years, many of the popular characters became 'stock' figures, well-loved and instantly recognisable by their 'fans'. Actors playing these roles, were able to explore and develop the popular characters through improvisation. However, these characters were no cardboard cut-outs, but breathed passion and fire. As a result, their feelings were often over-riding, resulting in 'sensation' taking over from objectivity. (See pages 160–162.) The most familiar of these characters to us, today, are Harlequin, Columbine and Pierrot, each the embodiment of very distinct personal characteristics: Harlequin was always the agile, irrepressible extrovert while Pierrot, the white-faced clown, though also agile, was the sad drooping lily. Columbine was the pretty, pert girl whom all the men fell for. But let us take eight of these commedia figures and examine their characters and which of the eight Basic Efforts apply to them.

**Harlequin.** A clown, well-known for his diamond-patterned suit. Compact in person, he is a lovable rogue. Bouncy, full of tricks and capable of violent movement, he can be insolent, mocking and ribald. A paradoxical figure, he can be brilliantly athletic or sluggish and lazy. Frequently disguises himself as other people and gets into scrapes.

*Efforts:* Flicking, Dabbing. Capable of Thrusting but sometimes Relaxes or Sinks.

**Columbine.** The soubrette, often portrayed as a lady's maid. She is young, pretty, coquettish, witty and amorous. All the men, however young or old, are attracted to her – a fact she takes full advantage of. She, too, is fond of diguising herself, sometimes as men!

*Efforts:* Flicking, Dabbing, Floating, Gliding.

**Pierrot.** A clown. Sometimes known as Pagliaccio, which will be familiar to opera-goers. This is a sad clown, who wears a loose, white blouse and baggy white trousers. Also his face is painted white with a woebegone expression. In spite of this, he can be very funny, particularly as he is extremely supple, as though double-jointed, and can move and droop about like a marionette.

*Efforts:* Gliding, Floating, with a lot of Relaxing and Sinking.

**Pantalone.** An old man. Very lean; everything about him is angular and pointed except for his paunch. He is usually rich and miserly and easily impressed by other people's wealth. Easily duped and gullible, he is typical of a rich old father who insists his daughter marries a wealthy man, however revolting he may be.

*Efforts:* Pressing, Dabbing.

**Doctor.** Another old man who is rich, and therefore a friend of Pantalone. Not really a doctor, but always wears black, the costume of doctors. His air of self-sufficiency and gravity conceals a shallow fraud. A veritable gas-bag, he constantly spouts Latin to impress people. Repulsive, with his creepy fingers, he ogles the girls in the vain hope that they will be interested in him.

*Efforts:* Gliding, Pressing.


**Pulcinella.** Later known in England as Punch. An old curmudgeon with a hump, and a large nose that nearly meets his nutcracker chin. He is sharp and witty but often feigns stupidity. Capable of being violent, his temper is alarming.

*Efforts:* Dabbing, Flicking, Slashing.


**Inamorata.** An idealised type of woman. Beautiful, cultured and charming, she has many passionate admirers to whom she seems unattainable. She is reluctant to reveal her own heart. Olivia in Shakespeare's *Twelfth Night* is a perfect example.

*Efforts:* Floating, Gliding.


**The Captain.** A braggart. He is bombastic, loud-mouthed, aggressive and swash-buckling, but considers himself a gallant slayer of hearts. Beneath the braggadocio there lurks a coward.

*Efforts:* Thrusting, Slashing. When the tables are turned: Dab-gliding, Float-flicking.


There are many other commedia characters but these eight are the main ones and their counterparts can be seen all around us today. There are plenty of bouncing Harlequins around, just as there are drooping-lily Pierrots and deliciously pert Columbines (was not Marilyn Monroe a perfect Columbine?), and just think how many people you know who would fit the characters of the Captain, or the Doctor or Pantalone. And maybe that coolly elegant lady who lives in the big house is an Inamorata. Who knows? These characters are a wonderful source to draw upon for all that is fine in the heritage of great acting.

# 9

# *For Those Who Dance*

What is dance? And how does it differ from movement? Can we define the difference in movement and dance? Where, for instance, does one become the other? It is a moot point.

The role of movement in everyday life is obvious; it is the essence of life, our very life force. Laban said that we move in order to satisfy a need. For example, reaching out for something we want, or getting from one place to another. These are basic, functional actions that we *need* to do and, more often than not, do not involve the emotions. Dancing *does* involve the emotions, which may be the reason that so many people are reluctant to let themselves go, in the same way that many people are reluctant to sing. The parallel between walking and dancing and talking and singing is well worth our consideration. Dancing could be described as an emotional extension of ordinary movement, just as singing is an emotional extension of speech. Indeed, we cannot sing or dance without the springboard of some emotion. If we did, the result would be horrible. Yet it is this emotional step that for many people proves more of a block than the lack of technique of either dancing or singing. Heightened emotion should make us feel the need to dance or sing and,

if we are not inhibited, not worried about making a fool of ourselves, we will abandon ourselves to it. On the other hand, a soldier on parade would seem to be far from feeling emotional and we would hardly equate his marching with dancing, though sometimes it comes very close to it! When the command comes to 'change step', the nifty skip-change from left, right, left, right' to 'left, right, *left*-right, left', is really in dance

   I     2     3    4      I    2   *and*  3    4

terms a 'step-ball-change'. In the unlikely event of the soldier continuing to 'step-ball-change' down the road, he would certainly be dancing!

Contrary to common belief, dancing is not confined to just legs and feet. One can dance with every part of the body, including the arms, neck and head. The main vocabulary of dance movements consists of hops, skips, jumps, kicks (both high and low), hand-clapping, foot-tapping, twisting, turning, stretching and arching the body. Many of these can be used in a purely functional way but they will be different. There is a great deal of difference in an ordinary turn and a pirouette!

### Hops and Springs

The childhood game of hop-scotch is a good example of hopping on one leg in any direction, springing on to the other leg and continue hopping.

● Spring in any direction either with two feet together, from one foot to another or, as in the diameters, from one foot to two and vice versa.

### Turns and pirouettes.

● 'Changing front' in the kinesphere is part of a dancer's vocabulary. The ballet enthusiast will be used to seeing the ballerina pirou-etting either on the spot or travelling across the stage. Her eyes only momentarily leaving their focus on her forward direction of travel. Although her personal space may change many times, she will remain aware of the audience and her 'front' in the general space of the auditorium. The turns are usually performed 'en pointe' (on her toes), in an upright position with a straight back. The dancer moves around a vertical axis, i.e. the high/deep dimension, linked to the Dimensional Scale. Ice skaters often spin on the spot from high to deep and vice versa using this vertical axis, although at the highest level they tend to arch the back and at the lowest, curl over forward to maintain balance. Often visually pleasing, these turns or pirouettes are usually stable in their executiion. For those students who have followed Laban's introduction to the Dimensional Scale and its stability, this comes as no surprise. (There are other turns which can be based on a diagonal axis and are more labile i.e.unstable.)

## Turning

- Starting position. Weight on the left foot. The right foot pointing to the right. Transfer the weight to the ball of the right foot and swing the body round to face the back wall, taking weight on the ball of the left foot as it arrives in another open position, completing a whole step (open to open position) and now facing the back of the room. You now have the option of returning the way you came or making the turn a complete one by continuing in the same direction ending in another open position. (In ballet terms, 'second position'.)

## Pirouettes

- i) Try turning continuously in one direction in a 'flowing on' manner. Use your arms to assist the turn. Try turning the other way.

- ii) After stepping sideways to the right to start the turn, the left foot joins the right foot for the turn. The right foot then moves sideways to start the next turn, followed immediately by the left joining it. Try pirouetting to the left.

## Leaps

- i) Run several steps before taking off from one leg, stretching the other leg forward before landing on it. Continue running and leap from the other leg.

- ii) Try leaping alternately from the right leg to the left leg, stretching the lifted leg as far forward as possible to cover distance.

If the lifted knee remains bent, the aim is more for height than distance. In all cases, experiment with the arms to assist the leaps. You will probably find the opposite arm to the lifted arm the most suitable.

- iii) Try the leaps doing a half turn with your body and then try whole turns.

## Dance Improvisations

- Improvise with very sharp angular arm movements in all directions, using your legs to leap, jump or merely run; the whole body will be involved in this lively activity.

● In contrast, now experiment by letting your arms lead the way in sweeping, wide-open angles, again with the participation of the whole body and using your legs to travel any way you wish. You can run, leap and turn, for instance. These movements are reminiscent of volutes and steeples described earlier on pages 101–103.

### More Dance Improvisation

● Try writing letters of the alphabet or numbers in the air with your arms, hands, head, body, legs and feet, creating imaginative shapes by introducing turns and jumps. Small, isolated body sections, such as hands and fingers, will make small letters; with the help of the whole arm, the letter will become much larger. The same, of course, applies to movements of the feet and legs. Involving the whole body with leaping and collapsing to the ground before rising again, can be very exciting to do and to observe. 1, 4, 7 and Z, V, W are examples of 'steeples'; 3, 6, 8 and O, C, S are examples of 'volutes'.

It is possible to use both 'steeples' and 'volutes' in the same letter or number. For instance, 2 and 5 or P and G. The movement shape can be vertical or horizontal or a mixture of both. Be absolutely clear what you want to do. As your movement 'mixture' becomes more imaginative and fantastic, it is more than likely that the original shapes will merge and the expressive qualities will be enhanced. The more fantastic and imaginative it becomes, the more it will lead you away from the original letter or number but the expressive quality should remain and will probably be enhanced. Before you know where you are you will have created a dance!

### Variation of the 'Flowing' 'A' Scale.

This variation is one of Laban's earliest and is on the threshold of being between an exercise and an expressive solo dance. Unusually strong counter-tensions occur along some of the movement pathways. Although the leading side (in this case, the right side) will have 'dominance' i.e. be emphasised, every attempt should be made for your left arm to reach towards its goal.

### Right Side leading

The pathways for the right side of the Flowing 'A' Scale remain the same throughout as does the rotation of the expressive qualities of the Table (flat), Door (steep) and Wheel (flowing) planes. **Bold type**, apart from a heading, indicates the pathways for the left arm. The bracketed numbers refer to Figure 40 on page 81.

● *Preparation:* Take a step back with your right foot crossing behind your left leg to the Left/Deep/Back corner. Simultaneously, take your right hand under the left arm to reach towards point Left/Back (12) of the Table Plane. **Your left leg is in counter-tension whilst your left arm points towards Forward/Deep (11).**

● *Pathway 1:* From Left/Back, take your right arm to point Right/High (1). Your right leg should step to the right (taking weight) whilst **your left arm moves into Left/Back (12),** just vacated by your right arm. The left leg remains in counter-tension to the right leg. **(The movement of your left arm will, from now on, always be one pathway behind your right arm, following the leading right side.)**

● *Pathway 2:* From Right/High, move your right arm along the 'steep' pathway to point towards Back/Deep (2), your right leg simultaneously stepping back to join it. The Back/Deep position lifts your left leg in its forward counter-tension position **whilst your left arm moves into the direction of Right/High (1).**

● *Pathway 3:* From Back/Deep (2) your right leg now crosses over in front of your body to Left/Deep/Forward whilst your right arm moves to Left/Forward (3) of the Table Plane. Try to keep facing front, inclining your body forward and your left leg (knee slightly bent) is in counter-tension crossing over your right side. **Your left arm moves down, crossing over the left side and points towards Back/Deep (2).**

● *Pathway 4:* Your right leg now moves to point Right/Deep (4) of the Door Plane. Try and bend your right leg as much as possible whilst your right arm also reaches to point (4). Your left leg is partially outstretched whilst your **left arm simultaneously travels as far as possible towards Left/Forward (3).**

● *Pathway 5:* The emphasis is on the movement of the right arm as it stretches to (5) whilst your right foot steps back to Back/Deep. **Meanwhile the left arm simultaneously crosses the body pointing in the direction of Right/Deep(4).**

- *Pathway 6:* As your right leg steps into Right/Deep/Forward and your right arm moves forward to Right/Forward (6), your left leg raised in counter-tension. Whilst the emphasis is on Right/Forward (6) and your body will be inclined in this direction, your **left arm will simultaneously have passed the right arm as it moved backward to Back/High (5). How far your left leg is raised off the ground depends on how far forward you are reaching.**

- *Pathway 7:* Your right arm and leg cross over to point Left/Deep (7) **whilst your left arm simultaneously moves over your right arm towards point Right/Forward (6).** The feeling will be one of extreme counter-tension.

- *Pathway 8:* Your right leg moves to Forward/Deep and your right arm to Forward/High (8) of the Wheel Plane **whilst your left arm travels simultaneusly, opening out and pointing in the direction of Left/Deep (7).**

- *Pathway 9:* Now take your right leg out to Right/Deep/Back and your right arm to Right/Back (9). Your body will be inclined backward and your left leg raised in counter-tension **whilst simultaneously your left arm has moved forward and is reaching towards Forward/High (8).**

- *Pathway 10:* Your right leg now crosses to Left/Deep and your right arm to Left/High (10). **Simultaneously your following left arm passes underneath your right arm and points towards Right/Back (9). Once again, although the emphasis is on the leading right side, there is a tremendous sideways counter-tension.**

- *Pathway 11:* Your right arm and leg move forward to Deep/Forward (11) of the Wheel Plane. Your left leg is lifted in counter-tension whilst **simultaneously your left arm opens out to Left/High (10).**

- *Pathway 12:* From Deep/Forward your right leg crosses behind your left leg and takes weight as your right arm passes underneath your left arm stretching into point Left/Back (12), your body arching slightly over Left/Back. Simultaneously, **your left arm points towards Deep/Forward (11)** whilst your right leg provides a strong right counter-tension as your body is 'pulled' in the direction of a horizontal position.

- Try the whole scale through on the left side.

## Dance exercises

- Starting Position. The weight is on your left foot and the right leg is crossing behind the left in Left/Back, resting on the ball of the foot.

- Run on a diagonal line, taking four steps (Right, Left, Right and Left). On the 5th step fly high and forward into the Right/High/Forward diagonal.

- As you land on your right foot with your right knee in a deep bend position, swing the left leg to cross in front and round the supporting leg in a gathering turn with the left arm assisting the turn. (If you cannot manage the whole turn on one leg put the left foot down to help).

- Spin out of the (right) turn into running in a wide curve to arrive approximately behind your starting place.

- With a few preparatory steps forward, take off, exulting in flying high into the tetrahedral shape described on page 39. Keep the tension momentarily whilst in the air, before falling into a crouched position on one knee.

- Try the other side.

## Open Springs

- Spring from two feet in stance position and land on the right foot in Right/Forward with your knee bent. Your body should be nearly horizontal with your left leg stretched behind in counter-tension Left/Back (12). Your right arm is Right/Forward (6) and your left in counter-tension. You have moved into an **open position**. (Your right side leading the movement to Forward/Right.)

- Spring off the supporting right leg back into stance and make sure both feet land **simultaneously**, not one after the other, a common mistake with beginners. Your body should return to an upright position.

- Spring from stance and, this time, your left leg lands in the open Left/Forward position with bent knee. Your body should be almost horizontal in this position. Your left arm is Left/Forward (Left 6) and your right is in counter-tension in this open position.

- Spring back to stance, feet again arriving **simultaneously**, your body returning to an upright position.

- Spring from stance to Right/Back and with the right side leading, land on your right foot with the knee bent and your body as horizontal as possible. The right arm pointing to (9). Try not to turn the body. The hips should remain facing front in the open position. Your left arm is in counter-tension, pointing to (Left 6).

- Spring back to stance again, both feet arriving **simultaneously** and the body returning to an upright position again.

- Spring from stance to Left/Back with the left foot. The left side is leading in this open position. Your left arm is pointing to (Left 9) whilst your right arm is in counter-tension. Your body should be inclined towards the horizontal. Try to keep the hips facing Forward.

- Spring back to stance, returning to an upright position and landing with both feet **simultaneously.**

All these springs have been attempted on their 'open side', i.e. the right side leading to the right and the left to the left side.

### *Variant*

- From stance, spring to Right/Forward (open) landing on the right foot. Spring back to stance and immediately spring again to Left/Back (open) with the left foot. Spring, returning to stance.

- Spring to open position Left/Forward with the left foot and back again to stance.

- Spring to open Right/Back with the right foot leading and spring back to stance.

- Spring to Left/Back open with the left foot leading and spring back to stance again.

- Spring to Right/Forward open with the right foot and spring back again to stance. Repeat.

Remember to arrive simultaneously with your feet in stance.

### *Second Variant* (*keeping to the open positions*)

- Starting position. Open horizontal position Right/Forward with your right foot Forward and your body almost horizontal.

- Spring to land in open Left/Back with your left foot leading, (by-passing the stance position). Spring returning to Right/Forward.

This requires more effort as you start from a leaning backward position.

Repeat several times and then try starting with the other side leading and then repeat that several times.

### Closed (or Crossing) springs

The leading side of the body will be moving to its opposite side. It might be helpful if you look at the 'A' Scale briefly on page 81 for the position of the body and limbs crossing in the Table Plane.

- From stance, spring into Right/Forward with your left leg. Your left arm pointing to (Left 3) and your right in counter-tension. Spring, returning to stance.

- Spring to Left/Forward with your right leg. Your right arm pointing to (3) and your left is in counter-tension. Spring back to stance.

- Spring to Right/Back with your left leg. Your left arm pointing to (Left 12) and your right arm in counter-tension. Spring back to stance.

- Spring to Left/Back with your right leg. Your right arm pointing to (12) and your left arm in counter-tension. Spring back to stance.

First Variant. Remember these are all crossed positions.

- Starting position. Right/Forward with your left leg. Spring to Left/Back, by-passing stance.

- Work through the other three crossing springs from the Table Plane, as before, from the beginning but now by-passing the intermediate stage of 'stance'.

- There are many variations. Try alternately changing sides, travelling continuously forward (or backward on a diameter) as follows:-

### Travelling along a diameter

- Right side leading followed by left side leading. From stance, swing your left arm in a big curve from your body centre over the ground to open Left/Forward whilst your left leg with deeply bent knee takes 4 hops in that direction as your body is as horizontal as possible and remains facing Forward. Repeat to Right/Forward with your right leg.

- Try the same movement into the open positions backward.

- Try the forward movements crossing in front of your body.

- Try the movements travelling backwards, arm crossing in front of the body and reaching back.

- Try to touch the ground with your fingertips each time you describe a wide arc (the swing) with your arm and make sure you have a good counter-stretch.

- Mix the two exercises together; later adding half and whole turns.

Below are examples of **3-ring and 5-ring swings,** which are logical forms appearing in the structural organisation of space (which began with our kinesphere introduction). There are many more and the many forms are endless. These two examples are the briefest snippets of the movement treasures out there in the kinesphere and, who knows, beyond?

### Icosahedral 3-Ring Swings

Laban originally called them 'ring swings'. This seemed quite natural from the circular motion of the movement. Each segment of the 3-ring has a diagonal inclination. The ring is triangular in shape and is located round the centre. Each 3-ring has its counterpart.

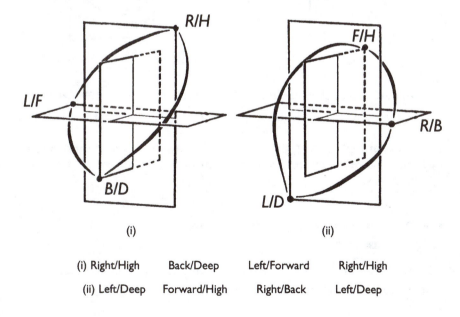

(i)                                    (ii)

|  |  |  |  |
|---|---|---|---|
| (i) Right/High | Back/Deep | Left/Forward | Right/High |
| (ii) Left/Deep | Forward/High | Right/Back | Left/Deep |

- Leading with the right side, work through each 3-ring precisely, taking one step in each direction This will again remind you of the flat, steep and flowing qualities of the three planes.

- Circle in a flowing, harmonious movement taking as many steps as you wish, involving your whole body in the 'swing'. Repeat on the other side. Later, you may wish to add turns.

### Icosahedral 5-Ring Swing

The peripheral 5-ring swings are the simplest forms of the rings. They are circular, moving through five vertices, each of which surrounds a planal corner. There are twelve 5-rings in all, belonging in pairs sharing a common axis.

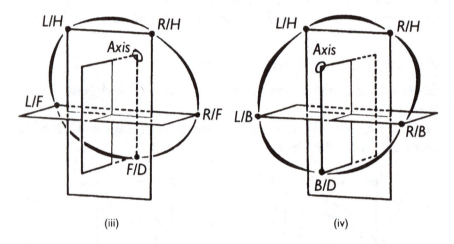

(iii)                                             (iv)

(iii) Circle around planal corner FH = L/H   R/H   R/F   F/D   L/F   H/L

(iv) Circle around planal corner BH = L/H   R/H   R/B   B/D   L/B   L/H

- Work through as with the 3-rings. You may wish to take more steps and explore the expressive movement pathways in each of the examples.

### Step Sequences to a Rhythmic Pattern
### (Rhythm and Co-ordination Sequences)

This is really going back to preliminaries but is nevertheless useful to re-assess. Note that the *italicised* words indicate extra weight:

## STEP SEQUENCES TO A RHYTHMIC PATTERN

- Take a count of 3 and walk it, a step to each count, as follows:

| I | 2 | 3, | I | 2 | 3, etc. |
|------|-------|-------|-------|------|-----------|
| left | right | left, | right | left | right, etc. |

- Hold the first step for two beats, making a 'lopsided' walk, the emphasis, or longer step being always on the left foot, as follows:

| I | 2 | 3, | I | 2 | 3, etc. |
|-------|---|--------|-------|---|-----------|
| *left* |   | right, | *left* |   | right, etc. |

- To make the previous exercise more interesting, divide the third beat into two half-beats and do a swift change of feet (a ball-change), as follows:

| I | 2 | 3 and, | I | 2 3 | and, etc. |
|-------|---|-------------|--------|-----|-------------|
| *left* |   | right-left, | *right* |     | left-right, etc. |

- There are many sub-divisions of the three beats that you can experiment with yourself. An interesting one is to step only on the first beat, hopping on the second and third beats with the same foot, while keeping the other leg raised high, as in the Ländler dance, based upon the action of treading grapes:

| I | 2 | 3, | I | 2 | 3, etc. |
|-------|------|-------|--------|-------|-----------|
| *step* | hop | hop, | *step* | hop | hop, etc. |
| *left* | left | left, | *right* | right | right, etc. |

- Take a count of four and walk it, a step to each count.

| I | 2 | 3 | 4, | I | 2 | 3 | 4, etc. |
|------|-------|------|--------|------|-------|------|-----------|
| left | right | left | right, | left | right | left | right, etc. |

- Hold the first step for two beats, making another 'lopsided' walk with the emphasis alternating from left to right, as follows:

| I | 2 | 3 | 4, | I | 2 | 3 | 4, etc. |
|-------|---|-------|-------|--------|---|---|-----------|
| *left* |   | right | left, | *right* |   | left | right, etc. |

- This time, hold the second step for two beats, making a 'lopsided' walk but syncopated i. e. accenting a weak beat, as follows:

| I | 2 | 3 | 4, | I | 2 | 3 | 4, etc. |
|------|--------|---|-------|-------|--------|---|-----------|
| left | *right* |   | left, | right | *left* |   | right, etc |

● Take a count of five and divide into even beats of 123, 12. Step on the 1 counts only, taking the weight as follows:

| 1 | 2 | 3, | 1 | 2, | 1 | 2 | 3, | 1 | 2, etc. |
|---|---|----|---|----|---|---|----|---|---------|
| *left* | | | right, | | *left* | | | right, etc. | |

Make sure the five beats are even. Do not feel tempted to lengthen the 1 2 into another 1 2 3. Again, the effect is 'lopsided', or asymmetrical, but in order to keep the movement flowing, make sure the non weight-bearing leg is always moving forward. As you get used to this asymetrical feeling, you can gradually involve your whole body, perhaps starting with leaning to the side the weight is on and extending the movement into your arms and head. The same process can be applied to the next exercise:

● Take a count of seven and divide it into even beats of 123, 12, 12. Step on the I counts only, taking the weight as follows:

| 1 | 2 | 3, | 1 | 2, | 1 | 2, | 1 | 2 | 3, | 1 | 2, | 1 | 2, etc. |
|---|---|----|---|----|---|----|---|---|----|---|----|---|---------|
| *Left* | | | right | | left, | | *right* | | | left | | right, etc. | |

A good way of trying out all these exercises is to sit down and do them with the palms of your hands on your lap. Once you are confident with the feelings of the rhythms, you can involve your shoulders and your upper body. From there you can stand up and let them take you where they will! Finally, take a count of eight and divide it into 1 2 3, 1 2 3, 1, 2 accenting the 1 beats. Try it at different speeds. You may recognise the fact that this rhythm is the basis of nearly all popular and rock music. The third beat of a normal 4/4 bar is pulled 'forward' to the two-and-a-half position, giving the staid 4/4 a kick!

## CHOREOGRAPHY AND MUSIC

Choreography, as we have observed, is the composition or creation of dances. Improvised dancing cannot truly be called choreography because it has not been designed and cannot be repeated. In other words, choreography is the composition of a specific set of movements which are usually performed to music – but not always. There have been dances choreographed to silence or to the beat of the dancers' feet or to hand-claps.

If the choreographer is going to use a piece of music, he has a much easier time than, say, fifty years ago. Now, choreographers have at their disposal an enormous wealth of recorded music to which they can listen at their leisure and compose their dances. With the help of cassettes and CDs they can repeat required sections over and over again until they are satisfied with their creations. They also have at their disposal, a sophisticated method of notation with which their work can be permanently recorded.

And how does a choreographer respond to a piece of music? Does he or she want to produce something that is pure dance or something with a story? Does the lyricism appeal to him or the exciting rhythm? Is the music dramatic or elegaic, savage or spiritual?

Rhythm is perhaps the first aspect to consider because it is the Time element upon which all else depends. Some music is much more obvious and simple in rhythm, such as a waltz or four steady beats in a bar. Other music may have a regular but uneven rhythm such as five or seven beats in a bar, or the rhythm may be constantly changing. Then there is syncopation, where the emphasis is on *off* or weak beats – it is interesting to compare dancers' response to a steady four beat rhythm and a syncopated four rhythm. The syncopation will nearly always generate much more freedom and flexibility throughout the whole body.

The *mood* of the music has to be considered and whether it has emotional content or not. It must say something to the choreographer who will pass it on to the dancers who should pass it on to the audience. Then there is the *structure* of the music: whether it builds to a climax or not; defining the shapes of the phrases – whether they are long extended melodies or short *motifs;* deciding whether the music is smooth and flowing or fragmented and spasmodic; finding what exists in the music that can be reflected in movement such as sequential phrases and antiphonal (question and answer) effects. Some choreographers may design their movements to harmonise with the shapes and rhythms in the music while others may prefer to work *against* the music as Nijinsky famously tried to do in *Le Sacre du Printemps* – a nightmare for the dancers. And, rather importantly, does the choreographer favour dancing primarily to beats or to the phrasing?

Today, choreography can be applied to many activities apart from dancing, such as synchronised swimming, aerobics, acrobatics and ice-skating.

In the theatre, the choreographer's role has changed over the years. No longer is his work confined to the composition of dances but it extends to what is now termed 'movement direction'. Actors are no longer left to their own, often haphazard devices but are given invaluable help in period movement styles, fencing (which *has* to be choreographed) and fighting. Choreographers can make wonderful set pieces by taking natural working actions, such as reaping, digging, hammering, washing and drinking (the list is endless) and stylising them into choreographic patterns. Scene-changes, where the movement of furniture and the carrying of props is visible to the audience, can be made into effective, almost dance-like sequences, transforming the mundane into something special.

A choreographer may be lucky enough to work with a composer, in which case, rather than being faced with a piece of music that is a *fait accompli*, the two can work in tandem, sometimes the composer suggesting musical ideas, sometimes the choreographer suggesting movements that inspire the composer. An ideal state of creativity.

## Doing a Dance

As a finale, let us take a well-known tune and celebrate with a dance. What could be better than some lively, well-known, music by Offenbach?

Here is a suggested choreography to the music, which is clearly in ABA format; if you don't like it, you can invent something yourself.

## Gallop step

Part A   Stance.

Bar 1    1. Take a half-step to the right with the right foot.

2. Hop on the spot with the right leg making a half-turn. (You are now facing the back.)

Bar 2    3. Take a half-step to the left with the left foot.

4. Close right foot to left in stance.

Bar 3    5. Take a half-step to the left with the left foot.

6. Hop on the spot with the left leg, making another half-turn to face forward again. (Turn back over your right shoulder so that you have made one complete turn in two halves).

Bar 4    7. Half-step to the right with the right foot.

8. The left foot follows with a hop (both feet momentarily in the air)

Bar 5    9. as the right leg moves again to the right (gallop).

10. Half-step to the right with the right foot.

Bar 6    11. The left foot follows with a hop (both feet momentarily in the air)

12. as the right foot again moves to the right (gallop).

Bar 7    13. Half-step to the right with the right foot.

14. The left foot follows with a hop (both feet momentarily in the air)

Bar 8    15. as the right foot again moves to the right (gallop).

16. Half-step to the right with the right foot.

Bar 9    17. The left foot follows with a hop (both feet momentarily in the air)

18. as the right foot again moves to the right taking weight (gallop). It resembles energetic sideways skipping.

Bar 10   19. Take a very small half-step springing to the left with the left foot, (close to stance).

20. Your right foot joins it, taking weight on the ball of the foot.

Bar 11   21. The left foot steps on the spot.

22. Take a very small half-step springing to the right with the right foot (close stance).

Bar 12   23. Your left foot joins it, taking weight on the ball of the foot.

24. Step on the spot with your right foot, taking weight.

25. Take a half-step to the left with your left foot.

26. Hop on the spot with your left leg making a half-turn. (You are now facing the back.)

27. Take a half-step to the right with the right foot.

28. Close left foot to right in stance.

29. Take a half-step to the right with the right foot.

30. Hop on the spot with the right leg, making another half-turn to face forward again.(Turn back over your left shoulder so that you have made one complete turn in two halves.)

31. Half-step to the left with the left foot.

32. The right foot follows with a hop (both feet momentarily in the air)

33. as the left leg moves again to the left (gallop).

34. Half-step to the left with the left foot.

35. The right foot follows with a hop (both feet momentarily in the air)

36. as the left foot again moves to the left (gallop).

37. Half-step to the left with the left foot.

38. The right foot follows with a hop (both feet momentarily in the air)

39. as the left foot again moves to the left (gallop).

40. Half-step to the left with the left foot.

41. The right foot follows with a hop (both feet momentarily in the air)

42. as the left foot again moves to the left taking weight (gallop). It resembles energetic sideways skipping.

43. Take a very small half-step springing to the right with the right foot, (close to stance).

44. Your left foot joins it, taking weight on the ball of the foot.

45. Your right foot steps on the spot.

46. Take a very small half-step springing to the left with your right foot (close stance).

47. Your right foot joins it, taking weight on the ball of the foot.

48. Step on the spot with your left foot, taking weight.

Bar 33  49. With your right foot take a stride in the open Right Forward direction.

50. Now your left foot strides to the open Left Forward direction.

Bar 34  51. Your right leg strides into an open Right Backward direction.

52. Now your left leg strides back in the open Left Backward direction.

You are now in a wide stance position with weight on both feet.

53. Accent the bending of the knees in this wide stance.

54. Accent the stretching of your knees as you lift your toes and balance on your heels.

55. Your right leg strides into open Right Forward direction.

56. Now your left leg strides into open Left Forward direction.

57. Your right leg strides again to the Right Backward direction.

58. Now your left leg strides to Left Backward direction.

59. Accent the bending of the knees.

60. Accent the stretching of the knees as you lift the toes and balance on your heels.

61. With your right leg take a stride to open Right Forward direction.

62. Now your left leg strides into the open Left Forward direction.

63. Your right leg strides into the open Right Backward direction.

64. Now the left leg strides into the open Left Backward direction.

Part B

65. Accent i) the bending and ii) the stretching of the knees as you finish by lifting your toes and balancing on your heels.

66. Accent i) the bending and ii) the stretching of the knees as you finish by lifting your toes and balancing on your heels.

67. With your right leg take a stride to the open Right Forward direction.

68. Now your left leg strides into the open Left Forward direction.

69. Your right leg strides into the open Right Backward direction.

70. Now your left leg strides into the open Left Backward direction.

71. Accent i) the bending and ii) the stretching of the knees as you finish by lifting your toes and balancing on your heels.

72. Accent i) the bending and ii) the stretching of the knees as you finish by lifting your toes and balancing on your heels.

(Be prepared to transfer weight on your left foot.)

73. Take an acented and exaggerated small half-step forward with the right foot as in running.

Let your body lean forward and your arms assist with 'piston-like' movement (elbows bent) throughout these running steps.

74. Accented and exaggerated half-step forward with the left foot.

75. Accented and exaggerated half-step forward with the right foot.

76. Accented and exaggerated half-step forward with the left foot.

77. Accented and exaggerated half-step forward with the right foot.

78. Accented and exaggerated half-step forward with the left foot.

79. Accented and exaggerated half-step forward with the right foot.

80. Finally, accented and exaggerated half-step forward with the left foot.

With the body leaning backwards and the arms raised 'akimbo', fingers fluttering, maintain the exaggerated movements by lifting the knees as far as you can. Nifty steps and body action required.

81. Drop back on the right foot as it takes a half-step backward.

82. Drop back on the left foot as it takes a half-step backward.

83. Drop back on the right foot as it takes a half-step backward.

84. Drop back on the left foot as it takes a half-step backward.

85. Drop back on the right foot as it takes a half-step backward.

86. Drop back on the left foot as it takes a half-step backward.

87. Drop back on the right foot as it take a half-step backward.

88. Drop back on the left foot as you take a half-step backward.

89. Take a half-step to the right with the right foot.

90. Hop on the spot with the right leg making a half-turn. (You are now facing the back.)

91. Take a half-step to the left with the left foot.

92. Close right foot to left in stance.

93. Take a half-step to the left with the left foot.

94. Hop on the spot with the left leg, making another half-turn to face forward again. (Turn back over your right shoulder so that you have made one complete turn in two halves.)

95. Half-step to the right with the right foot.

96. The left foot follows with a hop (both feet momentarily in the air taking its place)

Part A

97. as the right leg moves again to the right (gallop).

98. The left foot follows with a hop (both feet momentarily in the air taking its place).

99. as the right foot again moves to the Right (gallop).

100. The left foot follows with a hop, both feet momentarily in the air taking its place,

101. as the right foot again moves to the right (gallop).

102. Half-step to the right with the right foot.

103. The left foot follows with a hop (both feet momentarily in the air taking its place)

104. as the right foot again moves to the right taking weight (gallop). It resembles energetic sideways skipping.

105. Take a very small half-step springing to the left with the left foot (close to stance).

106. Your right foot joins it, taking weight on the ball of the foot.

107. The left foot steps on the spot.

108. Take a very small half-step springing to the right with the right foot (close stance).

109. Your left foot joins it, taking weight on the ball of the foot.

110. Step on the spot with your right foot, taking weight.

111. The left foot now take a half-step to the left.

112. Hop on the spot with the left leg making a half-turn. (You are now facing the back.)

113. Take a half-step to the right with the right foot.

114. Close left foot to right in stance.

115. Take a half-step to the right with the right foot.

116. Hop on the spot with the right leg, making another half-turn to face forward again. Turn back over your left shoulder so that you have made one complete turn in two halves.)

117. Half-step to the left with the left foot

118. The right foot follows with a hop (both feet momentarily in the air)

119. as the left leg moves again to the left (gallop).

120. Half-step to the left with the left foot.

121. The right foot follows with a hop (both feet momentarily in the air)

122. as the left foot again moves to the Left (gallop).

123. Half-step to the left with the left foot.

124. The right foot follows with a hop (both feet momentarily in the air)

125. as the left foot again moves to the Left (gallop).

126. Half-step to the left with the left foot.

127. The right foot follows with a hop (both feet momentarily in the air)

128. as the left foot again moves to the left taking weight (gallop). It resembles energetic sideways skipping.

129. Take a half-step to the right.

130. The left foot follows to the right taking a whole-step making a half-turn.

131. The body completes the turn when the right foot steps again to the right and you face front once more. Legs are in a wide stance, weight on the right leg.

132. Take a half-step to the left with the left leg.

133. The right foot follows the left with a whole-step making a half-turn.

134. The left continues the movement to the left with another whole-step, making another half-turn.

135. The right foot takes another whole-step to the left, making a half-turn.

136. The left follows on with a whole-step to the left and another half-turn. End with the weight on the left foot.

If you wish, you could do more turns to the left in the same amount of time.

137. Swing your right leg directly forward, the foot skimming the ground and bend it as it circles backward to join the left knee before

138. kneeling on the right knee.

139. Head up to face your 'audience'.

You may have started by carefully studying the steps, line by line. But with increasing confidence, feelings of real enjoyment will surely take over. Dancing should be fun. A wonderfully expressive and liberating experience whether you do it on your own or share it with others. Dance should be part of our daily life. How wonderful it would be if each of us could ask ourselves, 'Have I danced today?' and the answer was, 'Yes' .

# 10

# *For Those Who Teach*

It was George Bernard Shaw who famously remarked, 'Those who can, DO, and those who can't, TEACH,' and, unfortunately, one has seen much evidence of the truth of this. However, it has to be said that there are many individuals who can't DO, and who can't TEACH either, just as there are those who can DO and who can TEACH brilliantly, as well. Such a one was Laban; what he did, he taught.

Though his education was sparse and short-lived (he was expelled from school for dancing the czardas!), Laban was a supreme example of how to teach. Mostly self-educated, he acquired extensive knowledge in many subjects and fields, any one of which he could have taught as a separate subject. But to Laban, they were not separate subjects but were inextricably linked into a great universal entity; just as art was linked to the sciences, and dance was linked to gymnastics, so man was linked to the environment. As a boy, he was often left to his own devices, but he was no sluggard; having a marked talent for drawing and painting, he was able to observe everything around him with a practised eye. From these observations he gained knowledge from every possible source, from people, from animals and birds; from paintings and buildings; from geographical formations and the elements, and later on, when his passion for movement and dance emerged, from the Ancient Greeks, in particular, Plato and Pythagoras. All this knowledge became the foundation of what would alter the course of dance in the twentieth century, and all this he would impart to his students who came from far and wide, some of whom would go on to become leading names in the fields of European and American dance.

To learn from Laban was like going on an exciting journey – a journey that would never end. His teaching followed nobody else's curriculum for, like other great visionaries, he was an innovator and followed his own path.

Like all good teachers, he was constantly learning himself, appraising, surmizing and trying out new things, and he was never afraid to learn from his pupils.

With a beginner, Laban would never impose his own preconceived ideas before encouraging the student to reveal his own potential; he would search for a strong point before seeking out any weaknesses. Having found the strong point, he would encourage it and build on it; often the weaknesses would disappear without the student ever feeling at a disadvantage. Not that he couldn't be a stern task-master. Often he would drive his students far past their expectations and they were willing to be driven. Many of them must still remember his urging, 'Go on, go on. Go further!' The scales, of course, were a tremendous and exacting discipline but not before the student knew how and why he was doing them.

It is inconceivable that Laban was ever bored and, in turn, was never boring himself; he was too interested in everybody and everything. Thus, he inspired his students to do the same – to observe and take note. He taught them to be self-sufficient and to *dare* to try. Often, he would make students *prove* for themselves the right way to do something, even going as far as doing it the wrong way, first. Perhaps most important of all, he had a wicked sense of humour and was not beyond a little devilment.

# Post Script

**The person who has learnt to relate himself to Space, and has physical mastery of this, has Attention. The person who has mastery of his relation to the Weight factor of effort has Intention and he has Decision when he is adjusted to Time. Attention, intention and decision are the stages of inner preparation of an outer bodily action. This comes about when through the Flow of movement, effort finds concrete expression in the body.**

Thus said Rudolf Laban and it is a testimony to his greatness both as a man and as a teacher that he inspired all who came in contact with him, not just dancers, actors, and those connected with the arts, but people from all walks of life. In writing this book, we sincerely hope that we have succeeded in imparting some of that inspiration to you.

# How to Make
# Your Own Icosahedron

## Preparation

Anyone wishing to further their understanding of the kinospheric 'scaffolding' and its links with human movement should acquire a 3-dimensional model of an icosahedron. This can be small or large; small, as made with matchsticks or drinking straws, or even large enough to move in. The easiest method is to use drinking straws, which can be threaded together with wool (actual thread not being advisable as it cuts into the straws). This is not very strong but can serve its purpose. A more satisfactory model can be made with wooden rods or dowelling(depending on the size), of which you will need 30 equal lengths. Into each end of these lengths a screw-eye should be screwed.

Whether using straws or wooden struts, three pairs will represent the shorter sides of the three Planes (Door, Wheel and Table) and should be differently coloured to identify them. We suggest white for the top and bottom of the Door Plane, blue for the front and back of the Wheel Plane, and red for the opposite ends of the Table Plane. If straws are used, select three pairs of three different colours from the rest. Use a darning needle to thread the wool through the straws. If using wooden struts,use string to tie the screw-eyes together.

Take a good look at the diagram of the icosahedron alongside which is balancing on the bottom edge of the Door Plane. The numbering of the vertices corresponds to Laban's numbering of the signal points, and should greatly facilitate construction.

252

## Preparation

Lay the coloured struts out on a flat surface as in the diagram alongside, which is approximate to their position in the icosahedron.

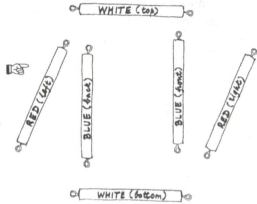

## Construction

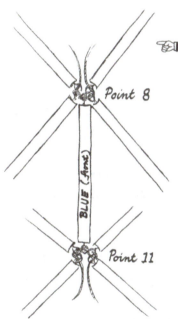

1. Take the front, blue strut and attach four plain struts to the top end (Point 8) and four plains to the bottom end (Point 11).

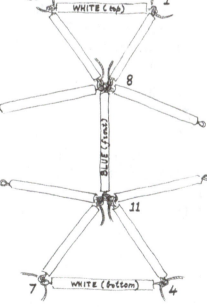

2. Attach the free end of the two inner struts at the top to each end of the top white strut (Points 1 and 10). Do the same with the bottom inner struts and attach their free ends to each end of the bottom white strut (Points 4 and 7).

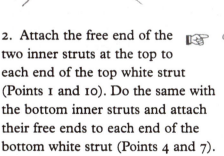

253

3. Attach both right-hand loose struts to the front of the right red strut (Point 6) and the two loose left-hand struts to the front of the left red strut (Point 3).

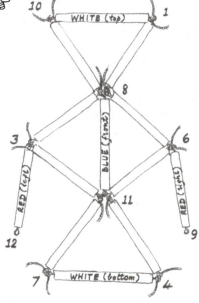

4. Now take the back, blue strut and repeat the procedure of 1: attach four plain struts to the top end (Point 5) and four plain struts to the bottom end (Point 2).

5. Attach the free ends of the two inner struts at the top to each end of the top white strut (Points 1 and 10) Do the same with the bottom inner struts and attach their free ends to each end of the bottom white strut (Points 4 and 7).

6. Attach both right-hand loose struts to the back of the right red strut (Point 9) and the two loose left-hand struts to the back of the left red strut (Point 12).

7. Finally, with the remaining eight struts, attach two to each of the Points 1, 4, 7 and 10. Then join Points 1 to 6, and 1 to 9; 4 to 6 and 4 to 9; 10 to 3 and 10 to 12; 7 to 3 and 7 to 12 and there you have it.

# Bibliography

Bodmer, Sylvia, *Harmonics in Space*, an article in *Movement and Dance*, Magazine of the Laban Guild, No. 71, November 1983.

Dalby, John, How *to Speak Well in Business*, Aardvark Press, New Mexico, 1993.

Freeman, Ira M., Physics *Made Simple*, Made Simple Books, W. H. Allen, London, 1967, reprinted 1971.

Hawking, Stephen, *A Brief History of Time*, Bantam Press, UK, 1988.

Hodgson, John, *Mastering Movement*, Methuen Publishing, 2001.

H.E. Huntley, *The Divine Proportion*, Dover Publications, New York, 1970.

Laban, Rudolf, *The Mastery of Movement on the Stage*, Macdonald and Evans, U.K. 1950.

———, *Modern Educational Dance*, revised by Lisa Ullmann, Macdonald and Evans, UK, 1948.

———, *Choreutics*, annotated and edited by Lisa Ullmann, Macdonald and Evans, UK, 1966.

———, *A Vision of Dynamic Space*, compiled by Lisa Ullmann, Laban Archives in association with the Falmer Press, London and Philadelphia, 1984.

Laban, Rudolf, and F. C. Lawrence, *Effort*, Macdonald and Evans, 1947.

Lawler, Lilian B., *The Dance of the Ancient Greek Theatre*, University of Iowa Press, USA, 1974.

Newlove, Jean, *Laban for Actors and Dancers*, Nick Hern Books, 1994.

Noverre, Jean Georges, *Letters on Dancing and Ballets,* translated and published by Cyril Beaumont, 1930.

O'Connor, J.D., *Phonetics*, Penguin Books, UK, 1973.

Preston-Dunlop, Valerie, *A Handbook for Dance in Education*, Macdonald and Evans, UK, 1980.

———, *Rudolf Laban, an Extraordinary Life*, Dance Books, Ltd., 1998.

For information about practical workshops
in Laban technique please write to Jean Newlove
c/o Nick Hern Books, The Glasshouse, 49A Goldhawk Road,
London W12 8QP. Also, signed copies of John Dalby's
illustrations
on pages 2 and and 167 are available for purchase:
please write to John Dalby, c/o Nick Hern Books, as above.